ADVANCE PRAISE FOR ....

Six concepts emerge for me:

1. **Relatable:** By that I mean that its 7 strategies can be useful if you are in sales or sales management. The stories used in the book are very familiar to those of us who are or have been in sales and sales management.

2. **Gestalt:** It is rare to find a book written that wants you to focus on the entire person and not just how to fix the business problems. (Sales - growth or management of people). It is unheard of to have a book that wants you to focus on the entire person- that is professional, personal and spiritual aspects.

3. **Courageous:** I challenge you to find business self help books in sales that encourage you to not dwell on caring what people think of you but instead care about what you think and do as long as it is true to yourself (that is where the integrity comes in). It takes courage to publically state that there are customers you do not want both as a salesperson and sales manager. In Chapter 7 this point is brought out when James talks of selecting only those customers who have potential and are sustainable. This focus on the long term and not the next quarter is radical in today's world. It also emphasizes that you need to

focus on selling value for both your customer and yourself. This is accomplished by not shrinking from your price. I am a college professor who has taught professional sales and sales management for almost 30 years and this book addresses many of the issues that students fail to grasp in their life. Honesty in being vulnerable and admitting that you do not have all the answers. Honesty in admitting and focusing on how work impacts your family as much or more that it impacts you. It is a rare and exciting to see a whole chapter (Chapter 10) devoted to the family and its importance to the entire process.

4. **Compelling:** This book is easy to read and honest. You can see the 7 strategies come alive in the way the book is written. His stories add a much needed honesty for the readers.

5. **Challenging:** The author challenges the reader to get out of their comfort zone. It reminds me of something I tell my students: What do you call the process of doing the same thing over and over and expecting different results? the answer is-Lunacy! James challenges each person to stretch their goals, expand your influencers (and provides suggestions on how to do that) and develop your personal brand. After all it is only he salesperson and sales manager that can provide sustainable value to customers and employees. I agree with the author in that a personal

brand is important and should be valued by the company and not feared. By having a great personal brand it provides more value to the customers as well as the company. The downside for a company is that it makes the person with a great personal brand very attractive (marketable) to other companies. The solution to reducing the fear of losing the person is to treat the person as a valued member of the team and not an employee.

6. **Motivational:** As I read the book I found myself wanting to get started to make the changes suggested by the author. The book lays out a simple but compelling way to reinvent yourself and your team to reach your stretch goals. Thus making life more enjoyable for yourself, your family and all those around you.

–DAN C. WEILBAKER, PH.D., *Sales Professor Emeritus,*
Northern Illinois University

Radical Integrity, the words so powerful together. I have so much I can apply to my sales process from this book. One of my favorite parts is about "setting the team up for success." The trick to growing your own sales team is by giving them the tools they need. *Radical Integrity* is powerful, valuable, and most importantly, actionable.

–JEFF J. HUNTER, *CEO, Branded Media*

This book is an excellent compilation of mindset, motivation, and strategy. Too often "sales" books are single sided, and leave the reader wonder "how to" implement the material in a sustainable way. This leaves many publications as material to reflect on by those that can truly put all of the pieces together in to actionable steps, like James prescribes. The fastest car in the world, without great tires and a skilled driver, can be out paced by a Miata.

The number of life changing steps exposed for the the reader to easily discern and put in to action places this book at the forefront of breakthrough development books in order to reach your own GREATNESS!!!

−**CHRIS WOOTEN**, *U.S. Marine Veteran*

One of my favorite quotes in your book is"The master will appear when the student is ready."

When you go into talking about creating a business strategy plan and knowing your customer, it is exactly what my team and I are working on right now. We just created an employee recognition program that went hospital wide and looking to go system wide, that I am ecstatic about!

What you discussed about creating your tribe is essential for any business and any group of people. That advice is immensely beneficial and I will absolutely be taking it back to my team for us to achieve our goals.

–EMILY JWEID, *Administrative Manager,*
The Mount Sinai Hospital

Radical Integrity is the epitome of author transparency, authenticity and real life strategies to yield success, regardless of your expertise and industry. James took me on the emotional rollercoaster of life, business and personal growth all in the first couple chapters so I was hooked! I found myself nodding "yes!" as he shared his struggles and allowed me to see the completely relatable side of being a spouse, parent, employee and entrepreneur all at the same time.

From sharing specific tools and strategies, actual scripts and examples for various sales and rapport-building scenarios, and incorporating written exercises, this is an interactive and highly engaging read for professionals of all industries and all levels. I'm incredibly grateful my mind was open to Radical Integrity and I'm excited to implement new strategies for success TODAY!

–CARRIE WOOTEN, *CEO of Mindset Enterprise*

RADICAL INTEGRITY

RADICAL INTEGRITY

7 Breakthrough Strategies *for* Transforming
Your Business, Sales, *and* Life

JAMES JACOBI

NEW YORK

LONDON • NASHVILLE • MELBOURNE • VANCOUVER

RADICAL INTEGRITY

7 Breakthrough Strategies for Transforming Your
Business, Sales, and Life

© 2020 James Jacobi

Published in New York, New York, by Morgan James Publishing in partnership with
Difference Press. Morgan James is a trademark of Morgan James, LLC.
www.MorganJamesPublishing.com

ISBN 9781642795134 paperback
ISBN 9781642795141 eBook
ISBN 9781642796186 audio
Library of Congress Control Number: 2019935742

Cover and Interior Design by:
Chris Treccani
www.3dogcreative.net

Morgan James is a proud partner of Habitat for Humanity Peninsula
and Greater Williamsburg. Partners in building since 2006.

Get involved today! Visit
MorganJamesPublishing.com/giving-back

I think of what the world could be

A vision of the one I see

A million dreams is all it's gonna take

A million dreams for the world we're gonna make

To my sons Grant and George, my daughter Willa, and my beautiful wife Lindsay, I hope this book and its results will inspire you to live your dream, no matter what.

TABLE OF CONTENTS

FOREWORD

Some people learn, a few will do (implement), and one percent of them will learn, do, and teach so that others may benefit and rise. James Jacobi is hands down, one of the one percent.

A couple of years ago I remember this young couple hopping on one of my training calls. Both were so ambitious, eager to learn, and willing to do whatever it took to win in life together. They did ALL THE WORK, they asked questions, applied, learned, and truly were cut from the greatest of character cloth. All would attest to that.

James was hustling in sales for a company who was so lucky to have his genius, and Lindsay, his beautiful wife, was hustling in sales online. They were hard workers, focused on their next level, and family values too. Yet, they had a dream and hopes of a bigger way.

Immediately, we all recognized their good hearts, great skills, and giving spirits. Not to mention their duo of talent, which was not even they fully realized yet. They were treasures in this world and teaching them to know the assets that they were, and how they serve others more by harnessing their talent, was the fun part.

Their story is similar to so many who have worked so hard for so long, who know they are worth more, and who know that just a few small adjustments would make all the difference. These two were willing to do the work to make it happen and this book just shows you how adamant they are about sharing it with all who are ready for the next level.

Lindsay and James were meant for greatness since day one. And it has been an honor to run with them and to now call them friends for life.

Now "James the Giant" emerged from a challenge (sorry James, you will never lose the nickname, for a legend, you rightly are.)

A few weeks into our mastermind, I do a challenge, a competition of greats and James emerged from the pack swinging with pure brilliance. Don't worry, the story is in the book. However, you must know that your finest results come from your greatest challenges, and if you are in one now, this book has arrived on time. James chose to rise. He chose to win, and it never stopped.

Fast forward, two years of hard work and complete commitment to the life they desired, both personal work and professional, James quickly became someone whom everyone looked up to. He was a creative, taking entrepreneurial skills and implementing them in the corporate world and winning big. All eyes were on him often to see what genius ideas he would bring to the table next. Some loved them, and some were frightened by them. Yet, every time he was making a difference for both customer/client and corporate team. He created win-wins consistently, never doubted his skills, and rose to the point where he no longer could watch salespeople lose, underachieve, or have unanswered questions again. He was to be the one to help. In a world where people ache for their win, he would be their answer.

James has gathered a wealth of knowledge from some of the greatest minds in the world, applied their teachings along with his own influence and character, and is now teaching it to help others straighten out their path to success. Now that's a leader! And it's all inside.

His story is one all will relate to, all will learn from, and one that will help to answer many of the questions that are key to creating lasting success in sales and in life.

This book is full of invaluable information. Read every single ounce of it and implement until it is a habit, and then move on to the next. There are hardcore truths which James knows are the only way to true success. I want you to take them all to heart for they will drastically change your results and future.

Beyond the book, please know there is so much more. This is the beginning for you. The starting point of learning. Do not stop here, for another treasure awaits you. I never just read an author, I study them, and I suggest you do the same. Connect with James, train with him, and learn what makes him a legend. I promise it will only get better. He is an investment well worth your time. So, begin here, dive in, shoot him a message on social, and let him know you are reading the book, and prepare to win. We all look forward to hearing your results.

And to James, you are the one your results require. Congratulations, and thank you for living your best life so others may live theirs. It's an honor to run with you.

Dive in friends, your next level awaits! And tell your others about it. They will be so grateful you did.

- Danelle Delgado

——

Why I Wrote This Book

I wrote this book to help millions of people in their businesses. Specifically, those who are sales leaders that are struggling to run the business, not hitting their sales, not seeing enough short-term wins and long-term gains/sustainability. It's for those who feel uncertain about knowing how to foster and grow a tribe or build the culture they want. It's for those who want to be a successful sales leader but are currently very challenged. I want to share my story of the last ten years and the strategies I learned along the way that have dramatically changed my life. I remember the days, weeks, and months where the grind was on, but it was like running on a hamster wheel. It was basically insanity, hoping and expecting things to be different and better every Monday to restart the week, but always ending back at the same place or worse in a matter of days, weeks, or months. Having low confidence from lack of results or wins, people telling you that you're doing awesome when you know they are just trying to keep you encouraged to fight through it, your team quitting on you, and your bosses telling you your weak points (sometimes in not an ideal communication style) all sucks. It sucks when you're not winning at work because that stress carries over to home. Your wife sees it. She wants better for you and more for you. She knows how much you care, and how hard you try. It's hard to raise your new/young kids on top of all this stress, uncertainty, fear, worry, and anxiety. There has to be a better way somehow. And there is. I promise you.

It took me five years, but I'm telling you it can take as little as ninety days to see major shifts that lead to big results and breakthroughs for you. And these are the strategies I want to share with you in this book. I break down into seven steps a system of how to become the most successful sales leader you can be, that you were born to be. Because you were *born* to be *great*. You are *great*. You have it in you. We just need to work on you finding it and bringing it out. It's there. You need to learn some things, change some things about yourself, to become the person you want to be. But it's very doable, and possible if you're serious. And, it won't take long. I'm telling you in ninety days you will make major leaps to where you want to go and who you want to be. Will you take that journey with me? You have to be serious about it, or it won't work. If you read this book once and just expect to change by osmosis, it probably won't happen. It takes daily practice and implementing the things I will teach you. But there are digestible little things that will move mountains in your life. It may seem strange, but the simple things actually hold tremendous power for the results you want. I assure you they are not complex problems you need to solve.

What if you read this book and worked with me for ninety days, and your sales grew by 400%? Or what if you landed your dream client that changed everything about your sales quotas?

What if you didn't lose another person on your team because you knew for sure that you were a strong and trusting leader that your team would follow anywhere until the end?

Can you imagine what you could do with the heart of your team behind you?

What about at home, can you imagine coming home day after day, week after week, and your wife seeing the joy and excitement on your face?

What about your little ones?

To be able to pour into them the same strategies you're using at work, and have your family quality life grow 400%?

This is all possible my friend. Your life, your lifestyle, your mood, your experiences, can be *awesome*, on a daily basis. I'm not saying your problems will never go away, or you'll never to have to grind hard again, or anything like that. Let's get real, work ethic, excellence, discipline are all required to be great and see results. But these strategies will work and help you become the successful sales leader you want to be.

And that's why I wrote this book. Because I lived all the bad to the point where I was a few questionable decisions away from catastrophic life damage. I was in emotional disarray, couldn't hold my team together, and tried everything but couldn't get sales up. My marriage and finances were stressed to the max, and my children got the worst of me when I came home because I couldn't deal with my stress and anxiety. I showed frustration, anger, more frustration, stress, worry, and none of those things were helpful to my family as a dad or husband. Something had to change, and it had to change fast. I chose to fire myself and start over.

All this, from the seven-step system I am about to share with you and to the world, for the first time. I wrote this book because I want to stop being selfish. I have a gift, a story, a solution, that I pray and hope will help millions of lives and families. I decided to write this book and not return to a corporate job, because that would be selfish. You wouldn't get me and my time, to help you. I am yours if you will have me. I want to help you win, and for you to become the sales leader you were born to be. You are great, and you are just a short time away from living your best self yet. I am beyond thrilled and full of gratitude that you are reading this book and considering what it can mean for your life and your business. I hope you truly take the time to soak this all in, to work on it. As Gary Vee would say, focus on the micro hyperactivity, along with having macro patience. Clouds and dirt. You have a massive role to play in many lives, and this time in your life is the time to level up, become the sales leader and person you were born to be, to help your business, teammates, family, and many more.

CHAPTER 1

Welcome to Sales ...
Leadership

If They Only Would Have Told You It Would Be Like This...

The last couple of years have been a whirlwind. You ground it out hard as a sales rep, learning and failing and winning and finding a way to succeed. You became a top producer along the way, all the things the company wants you to do - growing sales, leading and motivating your team. You're on your way up! Then you get promoted to your first management position, and it's a brand-new ball game for you. Lots to learn, lots to absorb, but you're excited. It's the job you've wanted for a long time and it's finally yours.

You've been a sales manager for several months now and it's all new. It's like moving into the majors (or the upper echelon of your favorite sport). If you were in baseball, the pitches would now be coming at you at 95 mph, when you were used to pitches at 60 mph. Your decision making needs to be faster. You have multiple people coming to you with problems simultaneously throughout the day. You listen and assist the best you can, but emails are piled up and you're pulled in ten different directions. Meanwhile, corporate is trying to reach you to talk about initiatives and your coworkers. It's a constant relay race, communicating what's happening on the front lines, and reporting it back to home base (corporate).

First House

Life happens too, right? You found that special someone, dated, and got married. You did the typical "live near the city" lifestyle to have fun nights and weekends with friends. Once you got married, you noticed your circle of friends changing, your needs changed. Then you had your first kid, and then life really changed! You had to make the move to the suburbs, find a real house, not an apartment. You need space for your growing family. You don't have enough savings, so you have to get help from your parents and do a first-time buyer FHA loan. None of your old friends know about changing diapers, nightly rituals, sleepless nights, new financial challenges, or new priorities, and your available time really starts to shift. All the while, you're in your leadership position and trying to figure out how to be ultra-successful at your job. You want to be the best, to have the most sales as an office, to have your teammates win and grow, to have money coming in so you can go home to your wife with a smile instead of frustration from the day, and to provide security for your family.

It's Sunday night and you just searched in Google: "how to be an effective leader," "growing sales," "managing a team," "how to budget," "happy marriage," "working dad."

You're just finishing up binge watching NFL Redzone, checking your fantasy teams, and planning your week out at your business. Your checklist is massive and daunting, you have tons of 1-on-1 weekly staff meetings, calls with corporate, several client meetings, a few internal interviews, some possible time for a few sales calls, an industry nightly event, and that's it. Your schedule is maxed out. Once you get going, you know it's a fast-paced week with little to no downtime. You feel like you're spending time in all the right places, but if it's like the last several weeks or months, something is missing. Revenue isn't going up. It's flat or going down. Or maybe it spikes but those spikes aren't sustained. You can almost predict that you'll have 1-2 quits or fires per quarter, though you're just not always sure who it will be. You know what kinds of conversations you'll have with upper management and the questions they'll ask you about what's happening in your office. You really do want to be great at your job. You care about your people. You care about your clients and your company, but it just seems like there're more failures and disappointments than successes and long-term sustainable growth. This leads you to search for articles, books, and YouTube videos. You find some great content, take notes, and can't wait to implement it tomorrow with your team. You wake up Monday, pumped, excited, and optimistic for a great day and week. You walk into your office, smile, and greet your team, and then one of your lead sales guys comes up to you and says, "Hey, can I talk with you for a minute in your office?" He politely quits, your house-of-cards collapse, and there go your grand plans and excitement for the week. Monday morning it's like "a case of the Mondays" from the movie *Office Space*. Your mood shifts, and now you think, "What the heck do I have to do to help my team win and grow this business?"

Your Pants Don't Fit

When's the last time you went to the gym? Maybe you go several times a week to get de-stressed. But how's your eating, and drinking? Yeah, you know. Work out super hard, feel awesome and jacked, but then you gladly binge eat pizza, burgers, wings, Mexican along with several drinks from Friday to Monday. And don't forget those lunches and client industry events during the week where you said, "I worked out today, I can cheat a little here and be fine." You look in the mirror every morning and are not happy with where you want to be, so you work out harder, but you don't really change your eating, yet expect something magical to happen. Then the worst thing possible happens. You are out during your week at an industry event, you bend over to pick up something you dropped, and your pants rip! It's the ultimate "OMG I'm fat" moment. Your self-image takes another huge blow, but rather than make the routine statement, "This is the final moment, I'm going to change once and for all." You pledge to start a massive diet and workout routine tomorrow. But for tonight, you have a few drinks to wipe away this depressing moment.

The Weekend Budget Talk Ritual

You know exactly where I'm going here. Yeah, the paycheck hits Friday and it's underwhelming. You have your weekly mortgage due (because you can't afford to pay it all at once from a cash flow perspective), your phone, internet, gas, water, cable tv, two car payments, and two car insurance payments. You want to go out to dinner at one of your favorite restaurants with your wife because you want to de-stress and enjoy a nice meal. Oh wait, there's the student loan payments, medical bills from your labor, delivery, and fertility meds, plus your credit card minimum payments. Yep, then you get to dinner and your topic of conversation: the budget. How do we get out of this? Your wife asks you how you will make more money at work. Where can you cut back in your expenses, if at all? Your in-laws who come over weekly chime in and try to help, but also talk about the issue ad nauseam. And just like that, your weekends are no longer relaxing, instead, they are a 48-hour mountainous mental hike of "how will I turn things around on Monday and get to where I want to be with my career, my finances, my team?" This is e-v-e-r-y single weekend, for months or years.

My eye is starting to twitch just talking about this and reminiscing. Yeah, the stress of this alone is one of the key reasons people divorce by the way. Money and finances. The truth is that you never had to really budget when you were single or even engaged. But as life grew and your family grew, so did your expenses and lifestyle preferences. No one wants to live poor, stay poor, have no toys, not do anything fun, or not go on trips/vacations. You want to prosper for your family and business. You want to have the typical story of climbing the corporate ladder, seeing the stages of success and money and influence and impact continually increase.

But they're not. Your health isn't showing it. Your bank account isn't either. And you've now legit thought about doing UBER or starting a side hustle to just make it.

The Boss Conversations

Hopefully you're fortunate to have a great boss who is super helpful, is a great mentor, and teaches you how to be great, and it's working. But this just isn't the case for most. There are parts of your boss that you admire, but there's more you find yourself complaining about to your close friends outside work over beers or to your wife during your "how was your day" conversations. It's almost always a drama when you share it with others. You got thrown into your sales leadership position, a sink or swim environment. You get to travel to headquarters quarterly and get a firehose two-hour training session on leadership or management, along with the twenty things they want you to implement when you go back, and then it's up to you to figure out how to do it.

Then, you have weekly calls with your boss to talk about how the implementations are going, what revenue you're expecting to drive, who you're hiring, and any stucks you are having. It's built and set up to be supportive, the intentions are good, but it just doesn't work for you. You occasionally have some genius ideas or solutions that you want to try, but they get shot down from your higher-ups. From your executive team, you may have even gotten, "We're sorry, we should have trained you more and knew it, but didn't. We're going to be better." And you take that apology, but secretly blame them for your shortcomings. I mean, you have the drive, the intent, you work your butt off until you can't open your eyes every day, but it doesn't add up to massive success for you.

At the end of the day, you have your scorecard. You're held accountable too for your revenue performance, hiring, implementing effective initiatives from above, and other things. And you haven't hit your scorecards often enough to get that next salary raise, bonus, and title. You are on an island with no support, no help, no direction. You are literally on the TV show *Lost*.

The Office, Your Weekly Drama Sitcom

No, I'm not talking about the TV show. I'm talking about YOUR office! Unless you're Steve Carrell, who is hilarious, your office is no laughing matter. Your livelihood, family, and career are at stake.

You have several people underperforming and have to train new hires at the same time. You find yourself spending all your time with these two groups, and it's rare you're spending any with your best people, which is what you've read in every leadership book not to do. There's always drama. This person doesn't get along with this person. This person is bringing their personal life into the workplace and the energy suck is felt at the office. You have some great-hearted teammates, but they lack confidence in themselves to do the job almost on a daily basis. They try and try, but never seem to find the level of success they want or need in their paycheck. You get out to happy hours and have a good heart-to-hearts with your team. You listen, you support, you encourage, you teach, but it isn't enough. You drive forty-five-minutes home and you're mentally, emotionally, and physically exhausted.

How can you get out of this continuous cycle of mediocrity, stress, and lack of progress? Don't get me wrong, there are moments of great wins and celebration. But it's a vicious roller coaster, and there seem to be only a few ups with mostly downs. You feel like your team, for the most part, is giving their all, and they look exhausted too. You know some are on the verge of quitting and will. You've seen this tape before.

Is it too much to ask, too high of a mountain to climb, to want to be a great leader and have success? Your intention to grow your sales team so they can all make more income, prosper, and grow is awesome. You know your team has massive student loans to pay, and their paychecks barely make it past rent and that alone.

Your marriage is stressed too. Your wife is taking care of your baby all day, hoping for and relying on you to come through. You want to be able to tell your wife that you can dream, you can save, you can go out to a nice dinner and not worry about it. But none of those things are happening. Where do you start? What do you fix? Help!

Ok, that's a lot of life right there and maybe it didn't exactly happen for you that way. But can you relate?

I want you to know and understand, that I connect with you. I can relate to you, whatever it is that you're going through. I've seen it all (or at least I think I have). I assure you, you are not alone. These challenges can be overcome, and you're on the brink of learning a system that will change your life forever. I welcome you with safety and honesty, to continue this book and let me help you move through this.

If you are ready, really ready, to make significant changes in your life that will have a profound positive difference, then what will follow will really help you. It wasn't until I let my ego really go, throw down my shield of pride, and my breastplate of insecurity, where I could let my heart be reached and start to be transformed. But as you will see, being vulnerable actually builds tremendous courage, integrity, trust, and freedom. Imagine knowing for sure, without a doubt, that you can successfully lead your team, they buy into you, you can make it rain with sales and business, and you're the happiest you've ever been at home with your spouse and kids?

Want to know something? Your family is ready for you to make this decision. They want it for you, and they need it for them. Your staff is ready for you to make this decision. They want it for you and need it for them. If it wasn't a little painful, everyone would do it. But the pain is short term, and the rewards are huge. I doubled my income, didn't lose a single person on my team in 2 years, build my largest book of business, got in the best shape of my life, found God again, and took my marriage to a whole new level of awesome from these strategies you're about to learn. Don't believe me? Let me share a little about what happened to me...

CHAPTER 2

I've Been There, Too

My Story and the Journey in Front of You

I remember when I started in sales, in a pure individual producer role. I was awful at it. I mean, I thought I was decent, but my results were awful. I worked so hard too, did eighty-hour work weeks, came in every Saturday and worked all day. Even when I met my wife Lindsay, which was six months into my career, she watched me work most of the weekends and late nights. It drove her, our friends, and her family nuts. Ever get told, "you don't need to work that hard?" I just had this belief that with enough time and pressure, something had to give. Eighteen months later, I was nowhere. I was hitting all my activity numbers too, meetings, calls, etc! I was ready to quit, which I don't do because I'm very stubborn and competitive. I want to win at anything I do. But life was happening, and I needed to pay for a ring, a wedding, and more rent for a bigger apartment, so something had to change. I finally faced myself, became more self-aware, and looked in the mirror. I knew exactly why things weren't working: I wasn't asking for the business in my presentations to clients. I was continuously meeting prospects that I knew to my core would never buy or didn't qualify as a good prospect. I did it to hit my quotas, to not lose my job. I was too lackadaisical with my time. I didn't treat it as precious. I gave it away to anyone just to be friendly and helpful. I was the ultimate team player and cheerleader for others' success, but not for my own. I wised up, made all those changes and six months later became the number one sales person in my company. Then I got promoted to sales leader. With the sales role, I was able to self-manage out of that and find a way to win. However, with the leadership role, the climb was too steep and too high for me at the time to sort out, especially with being a leader, husband, and dad with so many responsibilities. I had too many things pulling me in too many directions. I was lost, overwhelmed, burnt out, stressed out, overweight, miserable.

I Fired Myself

Yep, I did. I had too much integrity and care for my people and business. I realized that I needed to take a step back in order to move forward one day. I needed time to learn things I was missing, regroup, rebuild myself into something new. A new, and better version of myself. Most people will not do this, it takes balls and lowering your pride and ego to let go of the throne. No more executive board room meetings at HQ. No more pow wows with your peers in leadership. No more access to higher stock options if you perform well, and likely a very difficult path to rise to executive leadership someday as I took myself out of the natural path to get there. Yeah, that is a gut shot. But at some point, you have to say to yourself, enough is enough. I could not watch my family and staff suffer through whatever the mess that wasn't working for our business and life. I left the state, moved back to New Jersey where my wife is from and where my career first took root. I was asked to open up a new line of business for the company and get a new team to work with. Small at first, just one person, but as I scaled the business, I was allowed to have more staff.

Cue Your Favorite Intense Epic Soundtrack

What's your favorite motivational music? I have several genres. For whatever reason, I went to epic action movie soundtracks. Mine was the soundtrack from a Jason Bourne movie. I was back in New Jersey with a fresh start. The world was my oyster, and the sea of opportunity was abundant. After the first month of doing market surveillance, I was getting even more excited as I learned the market for my target client was 10x the size of my previous market. It was time. I was on a mission to crush it, dominate, and prove that I could skyrocket sales and build this business. And I did. In three months, I went from a $0 book of business to a book with a run rate of $1.5M in revenue. Most salespeople take eighteen to twenty-four months to achieve that, if ever. It was a shock and awe insurgency of sales activity and big spikes of revenue growth. It was exciting. I got a second seasoned teammate, so our wolfpack grew to three.

Cue the Epic Fail Scene When the Hero Loses It All

Yep, then literally not even two months later, everything went down the drain. One of my teammates at twenty-four –years old, went blind from a rare disease. He was a division 1 athlete in college, completely ripped with no body fat on him. He was very healthy and had an impeccable diet. Yet still, he became susceptible for a rare disease. It was the hardest thing to watch. He is one of the most stand up guys I've ever met or worked with. All he wants to do is serve others and help people, totally genuine and kind. My other teammate, Dylan, is a very large human of 6'6 and 260lbs. He managed to rip off muscle from his leg playing softball and was sidelined at home. The old days of highly competitive football and softball caught up with him. On top of that, the sales pipeline dried up and I couldn't close a darn deal. I remember going to my boss and saying, "I literally met thirty-one new customers and closed one in the last thirteen weeks." What can I do to improve? He said, "I don't know, maybe get a book on closing?" I knew right then that I had to take accountability for my results and go find help, wherever it may be. It wasn't available in the way I needed it where I was at. That didn't stop me from finding it though and winning.

Grant Cardone's 10X Conference and My New Success Coach

Never heard of this man before? I saw him on a YouTube video and immediately was intrigued. It led to me binge-watching several videos, and then I found out he was hosting an elite sales conference with top performers and speakers. One of them was an up-and-comer herself, Danelle Delgado. In just two years, she built a multi-million-dollar business after battling through cancer, getting divorced, and raising three small children on her own. Her client success stories were also impressive, enough for me to be convinced that my wife and I should hire her. My wife does direct sales for a little girls clothing company. Amazing product, but she was struggling too in building her team and her sales. Skip ahead a couple months and we were both being coached by her. We were on weekly calls and doing tons of weekly homework. I also took a trip to Bora Bora that cost everything I had during this time, but I'll get to that later in the book and what's important about that.

Ninety Days Later

I landed the largest account in my ten-year career and the largest in the history of the company for a single site field office. It was a $9 billion-dollar company in Manhattan, and they were number one on my desired client list of 500 that I made on day one when I moved back to New Jersey. My sales grew by 400% in a matter of weeks and lives were changed. We now had a run rate of $7M and climbing. BOOM! My teammates were jacked, and by this time, we were able to add another staff member, Danny. Our wolfpack grew to four. This team was different from all the rest I've ever worked with. We had a mission. We were certain we'd win. We had confidence beyond imagining and we were closing deals left and right. Our clients loved working with us, and we loved working with them. It was like a perfect dream story - the ideal client who valued and appreciated you, and you them, and your solutions were dramatically helping them win at their business. Isn't that what we're trying to achieve here? I had built the best tribe ever and didn't lose a single person in what is considered a high turnover industry. I remember looking at my paystub in April, and it was more total income than I had made all the year before. I was so excited, incredibly grateful to the point of tears, for the transformation that happened inside of me that brought out the desired results.

Impact to My Personal Brand

I discovered my personal brand and started to build it. I overhauled my LinkedIn page, started a new Instagram page, and got more strategic with my Facebook page. As I'll soon show you, personal brand matters. People buy from people they know, like, and trust! Yes, your company brand is important, but it's the people and their brands that build and shape it to what it means and stands for in the marketplace. While all the success at work was happening, I was also appointed to two board positions in the community. One for a nursing association that correlated with my line of work, and the other as one of the first millennial leaders to be on the Regional Chamber of Commerce Board of Directors. I was sitting in rooms with CEOs of every major local big and small company, the leading banks, the leading energy companies, the leading tech and biopharma companies, and me. It was very humbling and honoring to create a brand of integrity, energy, passion, authenticity, and professionalism. I was invited to Forbes HQ in Manhattan and attended a private launch party with Dr. Josh Luke, a healthcare futurist and industry expert. Things like this were becoming the new norm. I was even invited to speak at a business conference! Yep, and not just on any stage. I shared a stage with Tim Grover, the trainer of Michael Jordan, Kobe Bryant, and Dwayne Wade; Roddy Chong, the lead violinist for Celine Dion, Shania Twain, and Trans-Siberian Orchestra; and my amazing mentor and coach, Danelle Delgado. I got to tell the story I'm telling you now and advise hundreds of business leaders on how to massively grow their sales. It didn't end there. I was then invited to a Charity Gala and Business Accelerator Conference in Los Angeles. Without hesitation, I bought a plane ticket, arranged accommodations, rented a tux, and went.

I ended up meeting and interviewing the following people:

- Jack Canfield, author of Chicken Soup for the Soul, which has sold more than 500M copies
- Tom Bilyeu, CEO, and entrepreneur of Quest Bars ($1B company) and Impact Theory
- Tai Lopez, elite social media influencer

- Jason Sisneros, CEO of Anton Jae Global and owner of seven companies (aka The Bald Avenger)
- Brian Smith, founder of Ugg Boots
- Frank Shankwitz, founder of Make-A-Wish Foundation
- Paul Blanchard, president of Og Mandino Group
- Jeff Hoffman, founder of Priceline.com
- Ashton Kutcher, actor, and incredible investor, and entrepreneur
- Matthew McConaughey
- Dr. James Dentley, founder, NBC University
- Jay Samit, Vice Chairman of Deloitte and author of Disrupt You
- Jeffrey Hayzlett, founder of the Hero Club and C-Suite Network

You can see many of these interviews on my Instagram page: @realjamesjacobi.

You may or may not recognize some of these names. The point is that I was brought into levels of influence, success, knowledge, and impact beyond my former imagination.

Currently, I'm in mentorships with Ed Mylett, Chairman of World Financial Group, and Andy Frisella, MFCEO of 1st Phorm, Angela Lauria of The Author Incubator, Jason Sisneros of Anton Jae Global. Notice

I have several mentors. That's because I'm learning different skills from each person, who is a master of their own craft. I am also and member of the Hero Club with the C-Suite Network, a private club for CEOs with a mission for making a difference in the world.

Impact to My Family, Marriage, and Faith

My marriage and faith are on fire too! Lindsay and I took our marriage to a whole new level, many levels actually. One of the things I wasn't willing to address amidst all of this over the last several years was my spiritual life. You have a physical, emotional, and spiritual part of you. Imagine neglecting 33% of who you are for seven years or more. I got my act together and as the saying goes, "the master will appear when the student is ready." Well, thankfully through the providence of being in the Chamber of Commerce, I got to meet Pastor Tim Lucas who leads Liquid Church in New Jersey. It's one of the fastest growing churches in America, and I know why. Because he's doing the same thing that I'm going to teach you in this book.

Without getting too churchy on you, I'll just tell you that I have had a profound growth in my spiritual life over the last several months. Maybe the biggest is trusting God with His money. My viewpoints on money have changed, and I now give away more than I ever have in my entire life. I've seen increases financially, spiritually, and emotionally from the amazing service Pastor Tim and his team offer the community at Liquid. My family loves going to church, and faith is now a centerpiece of my marriage with Lindsay. It's been incredible, to say the least.

That all leads to the present. I came to a crossroads. I learned that I have so much to share and offer you and the world. It would be selfish of me to just stay quiet, not write this book, and take another corporate job. But I made the hard, risky, but easy at the same time choose to take the path of entrepreneurship in order to serve you. I am not encouraging you to be an entrepreneur in this book. I truly want to just help you and meet you where you are. I can help you become a highly successful leader in your company in a very short amount of time. In the following pages, I'm going to share with you how you can be a successful sales leader and achieve results like:

- Scale your sales by 400%
- Create an epic and strong tribe
- Double your income in twelve months or less
- Build a happy home life
- Create and grow your personal brand
- And more...

Are you ready? I'm so excited for you and grateful to be front and center of your attention. Thank you...

BONUS GOODIES JUST FOR YOU!

Go to **www.jamesjacobi.com/goodies** for secret access to 4 pieces of training on:

1. Taking the First Step - Becoming the Leader Within
2. Know Your Value - How to Become the Expert Your Client Needs
3. Show Your Value - How to Outshine Your Competition
4. Force Your Win - How to Have Unshakable Confidence and Close Business

If you want more help, book a call with me now. Just visit **https://JamesJacobi.as.me/**

YOU CANNOT FIND THIS PAGE FROM MY WEBSITE. IT'S A SECRET BETWEEN YOU AND ME, HERE. IT'S WORTH THOUSANDS OF DOLLARS, BUT FOR YOU IT'S FREE. I WANT TO HELP YOU WIN, RIGHT NOW, WHERE YOU ARE AT. YOU'VE GOT THIS! :-)

Now let's get to the good stuff. How did I pull all this off, and how can you learn the same exact system, and replicate it in your life, right now?

Let's get going...

CHAPTER 3

Your Roadmap to SUCCESS

"Our deepest fear is not that we are inadequate. Our deepest fear is that we are powerful beyond measure. It is our light, not our darkness, that most frightens us. Your playing small does not serve the world."

— MARIANNE WILLIAMSON

This is one of my favorite quotes because of how painfully true it is. We fear the greatness within because it would change everything. It would put you into uncharted waters. Change and the unknown are scary. You can and will be a successful sales leader, especially if you follow the steps that are about to be revealed to you in this book. You were meant to be great. You were born with talents and qualities that are meant to be shared and displayed for others. You were meant to be authentically you. And only you, no one else. Did you know that the odds of you being born are 1 in $10^{2,685,000}$. Crazy right?

The Truth About Where You Are, Right Now

The reason I bring this up is that we tend to admire those who lead us or influence us. The influencers in our lives are very powerful. But you are not them and they are not you. No matter how successful you become, you will reach a threshold if you are not authentically you. You cannot care about what people think about you. Maybe it's easy for you, maybe it's not. I made this mistake so many times in my career, whether it was staff or upper management, their opinion of me and their voice was more important than my own. When you read that and say it out loud, it sounds insane, but its true. And you have to start at the truth, where you are, right now. I will say it again, you must stop thinking or caring about what people think of you. It does not matter, I promise you. If you want to lead people, you need to lead yourself first. Do you want to know the truth of why you are not able to do all of the following:

- Scale your business to 2, 3, 4, 5x levels in a 6-month window or less

- Hit your sales quotas and see your team achieve their best performances ever
- Build a team of people that will follow you to no end (and won't quit on you)
- Build a strong personal brand in the marketplace positioning you to be an influencer
- Have an incredibly happy and awesome home life
- Be a remarkably successful sales leader

The truth is that the problem is you. You are 100% responsible for where you are at in your life right now. Every decision you have made has led to this point, this very moment you are reading this to yourself (or hearing it on Audible). That truth may hurt, and it should. Most don't really own their problems. They blame situations, circumstances, and other people instead. It doesn't matter if you think you have insufficient help from your leadership team. It doesn't matter how much or little training you've had to do the job you're in. It doesn't matter if you got dealt a bad hand of clients that yield your revenue. It doesn't matter if you inherited a team of people that don't exemplify your values or the company. It doesn't matter if it takes you eighty hours to do your work. It doesn't matter if you have precious time at home with your growing family. You may have really good reasons too, but it does not matter. You know the saying, "90% of life is how you react to it, 10% is what happens to you." I actually like how Ed Mylett teaches it, "where it's not happening to you, but for you." There's a purpose behind everything. If you can look at your life today and ask yourself, what am I supposed to be learning from this situation, this result, this conversation, this person? You are on the way, my friend, to incredible growth with this one shift in your thinking alone.

I'm bringing this up now, because if you do not accept 100% responsibility for your results and where you're at, and you aren't serious about changing your life to be a successful sales leader, then what follows will likely not bring you the results you desire. They could help, and should, but this is a pivotal point in your journey.

Are you ready? Do you really want to make changes in your life right now? This is a serious question. It's convenient to stay convenient, even if life truly sucks for you right now. What you have allowed in your life to this point is what you were willing to tolerate. What have you tolerated? You will face pain and hurt, and challenge, but that is only because you will be breaking down what needs broke down, and growing what will be required for you to become the successful leader you truly want to be.

Right now, before reading any further, get a piece of paper and pen. Write down the answers to the following questions:

1. What results do I want to achieve in my business and life in the next ninety days?
2. What results will I no longer tolerate for myself, my family, and my team?

The SUCCESS Process

Ok, great! In the following chapters, you will learn the SUCCESS process that guides you in achieving everything you just wrote down.

The SUCCESS process is:

Set your goals higher, much, much higher

Utilize and practice daily gratitude

Change your circles of influence

Catch fire your sales growth

Elevate your personal brand

Serve your people with radical integrity

Serve your family first, last, and foremost

You may not understand or see the point of some of these steps and how they translate to sales growth, better teams, and happiness. It shouldn't yet because you're not there. But if you just trust the process I teach in this book, you will find the treasures you've been seeking.

I've used these principles to get results. Mind you, it did not take me that long to see change. It only takes twenty-one days to form new habits, and not much longer to see significant changes in whatever you're implementing and executing. The SUCCESS process served me very well and it will serve you well too. The power in what you are about to learn will completely change your life if you let it.

Along with my travels in my journey to get here to you now a friend of mine, Helen a former executive who worked with Jack Welsh at GE, told me the following: "It's already done. You are already the success and person you want to be. Just remove the obstacles in front of you and become who you are." It's already done. It is already done. Declare that right now. Say it out loud, "IT IS ALREADY DONE." Now it's about taking action. Crash the boards! (As Helen has told me.)

Your future is yours and what you make of it. The door is open, time to walk through and become the successful sales leader you were born to be.

BONUS GOODIES JUST FOR YOU!

Go to www.jamesjacobi.com/goodies for secret access to 4 pieces of training on:

1. Taking the First Step - Becoming the Leader Within
2. Know Your Value - How to Become the Expert Your Client Needs
3. Show Your Value - How to Outshine Your Competition
4. Force Your Win - How to Have Unshakable Confidence and Close Business

If you want more help, book a call with me now. Just visit https://JamesJacobi.as.me/

YOU CANNOT FIND THIS PAGE FROM MY WEBSITE. IT'S A SECRET BETWEEN YOU AND ME, HERE. IT'S WORTH THOUSANDS OF DOLLARS, BUT FOR YOU IT'S FREE. I WANT TO HELP YOU WIN, RIGHT NOW, WHERE YOU ARE AT. YOU'VE GOT THIS! :-)

CHAPTER 4

Set Your Goals Higher, Much, Much Higher

Increase Your Identity

One of my favorite books of all-time is *The Greatest Salesman in the World* by Og Mandino. He talks about the secret scrolls. Scroll XIII is "I will multiply my value 100-fold." There are some key things that I want to share with you from this incredible author. Take a look at an excerpt from this text:

> *"First, I will set goals for the day, the week, the month, the year. In setting my goals I will consider my best performance of the past and multiply it 100x.*

To surpass the deeds of others is unimportant,
to surpass my own deeds, is all.
I will do the work a failure will not do.
I will always have my reach exceed my grasp.
I will never be content with my performance.
I will always raise my goals as soon as they are attained.
I will announce my goals to the world, yet I will never
proclaim any accomplishments."

I want you to think big, way bigger than you are now. Time to get out that piece of paper again. Let's do a short exercise here:

Using Og's recommendation, write down your goals for each category below. But first before you start, keep in mind that you are to look at your best performance in each category, and multiply it by 100-fold.

Day/Week/Month/Year Goals

- Business/Sales
- Income
- Team Growth
- Health
- Impact/Influence
- Family
- Faith

Get these on an index card and carry it with you everywhere. Ed Mylett taught me a strategy I like, where every time you lay your head down, put your hand on the steering wheel when you get in your car, get in the gym, walk into your office, think of these big goals, the big game you want to play. Do this as many times as you can per day. Essentially, the more often you can be thinking about where you are going, the less chance your mind will have time to think about anything else. Therefore, you'll only be looking for ways to get closer to where you want to go.

You have no time then for thinking and playing small, jealous thoughts, envious thoughts, hurtful thoughts about others, blaming or thinking ill of others' actions or behaviors, no matter how offensive they seemed to you, you must let go of all the negative. As Grant Cardone says, "No negativity allowed." Ever.

I remember one time where I noticed teammates talking negative about everything, and it started to become a daily habit in the office. I knew they didn't even realize how often they were saying negative things, things that seemed maybe insignificant to them, but were *huge* in framing and shaping their thoughts, feelings, and behaviors toward their business and others. I spoke to them and addressed it. I didn't come down on them, but encouraged them so they could do better, and explained why the words they were choosing to say were detrimental.

What is the big game you want to play? Have you ever given yourself the chance to even think about it? Put no limits on your thoughts here. Anything is game, anything is possible. How big do you want to play?

My goal when I started my new line of business two years ago was to create a $50M business in three to five years, grow and scale my team to twelve, become president of an association, and have world-class client satisfaction scores. They were very high goals, but big enough goals that they got me excited to aim for them.

Here's a quick test to see if your goals are big enough. After you have written them down say them out loud. Do that right now, real quick. Do your goals:

1. Get you really excited and inspired to go after them?
2. Give you a sense of awe and take your breath away?

If not, they may not be big enough. You need huge, big, gigantic goals for your life. Grant Cardone wrote an amazing book on the 10X rule. In it, one of the big takeaways I had was the reason people often fail is that they underestimate the work it will take to attain the goals they set out for. Don't let that be you. That's why you break your goals down to daily, weekly, monthly, and all the way to yearly and beyond. And put in ten times the effort you think it will take to achieve those goals. Learn and adjust every single day, as Og says, scale the mountain even higher tomorrow than what you did today. You will fail, its ok. But pick yourself back up and never, never give up.

I shared my goals with my team often. I told them how we would get there, or that I didn't know we would get there, but that we'd find a way, that it was possible. And when we hit our milestones, we'd take a picture of us crossing off that goal and moving on to the next. Just like the famous Bill Belichick for the NFL team the New England Patriots. After winning the Super Bowl, Belichick was already thinking and preparing for next season. He didn't stay content with his team's performance. I met a CFO that started his own consulting practice after being CFO at multiple companies for many years. He told me story after story about how he built businesses from scratch into $50M+ businesses, in a short amount of time (usually five years). It just reaffirmed to me that it is possible, it is possible for you.

Who cares what others think about your goals. Do not think about them or worry/wonder. The goals you have are not theirs, and they probably don't have the courage and tenacity that you do for even thinking that you can attain them. What matters is that you do better today than you did yesterday. And do not stop until you hit your goal.

In this program, we're going to focus on a ninety-day window (thirteen weeks, or a quarter for you in the business corporate world). I want you to have massive, 100x goals in the next ninety days. I do not care how ridiculous they may sound or seem, good! Make them audacious, ridiculous, laughable. You just have to have faith that you can do it, even though you may not know how yet. And even if you do pursue these goals and you fall short, it is better to aim high and land slightly lower, than to aim low, and then land even lower.

Map out your goals right now. What do you want to do, why do you want it, what will happen if you don't reach your goal, what will you do to celebrate if you do hit your goal?

I first heard of the ninety-day challenge from my success coach, Danelle Delgado. Her clients achieved massive results in ninety days, and you know what, I ended up being one of them. I had a hockey stick trajectory for my sales growth in those ninety days. It was the coolest looking graph I've ever seen of myself!

Believe you can, and will, land the biggest deals you can imagine.

Imagine that you can meet big influencers and take the stage with them.

Accept that you can lead a team successfully where they achieve their goals and potential.

Understand your why behind these crazy goals. What's the real reason you want to do all that you wrote down? You need to stay grounded, humble, and self-aware as you progress through this, or you will forget the purpose of why you started in the first place.

One thing that I've learned even recently from my book coach, Dr. Angela Lauria, is that every human wants to usually do both: not go for it and go for it at the same time. That's why building in accountability, as well as dates to complete your goals, will help you stay on track and not waver. Sometimes negative motivation is better than positive motivation. You definitely don't want to mess up and relive what you are living now, so that motivates you to do much better and improve your life.

All in all, aim high, very, very high. It doesn't matter what your corporate management has asked you to do. Go higher, go bigger, go all in. I'm talking go all in emotionally, physically, financially, spiritually. Burn the boats and say, "never again, will I return to where I once was." Taking action toward the future is the only way to get the results you want.

Be bold, be brave, announce your goals to the world, and set out to achieve them. Imagine if you had only one day to live, which is today. What would you do if you knew you only had one day to live and live out any dream you had? I will multiply my value 100-fold. Don't wait for something or some person to prompt you into this, take action today on your goals.

Your Rubicon Moment

Do you know what this means? I did not until recently at a secret retreat in the beautiful mountains of New York with fifty CEOs that are heroes. It's from Julius Caesar in ancient Rome. He was faced with a huge decision. He rose through the ranks and influence in his community, and he became a threat to the incumbent ruler Pompey and the Senate. It was treason to cross the river with an army, and Caesar did, which led to him overthrowing Pompey and taking the reins to start the Roman Empire as we know it today. The Rubicon Moment means the point of no return. I'm not saying to start a civil war with anyone, your company, your peers, or your family. But I am saying that this could be your Rubicon moment of authenticity. To be fully you and embrace all your faults and imperfections, and inner greatness that is ready to be unleashed. And in that regard, nothing is more important, no matter the cost. There is a point of no return when you decide to be 100% fully you, fully alive, fully authentic. Because when you do this, you open access to heavenly gifts, which are fearfully and wonderfully made in you. They will help you do things beyond your comprehension and make a difference in the world around you.

CHAPTER 5

Utilize and Practice Daily Gratitude

Your Foundational Beliefs, Thoughts, and Habits Are the Cornerstone

I turned over my team…4 times. Ouch! I cared, tried, gave it my all. They knew that too, but it wasn't enough. I clearly remember all the time I put into taking time out of the day to have 1-1 conversations with staff, hear what was on their mind, and see how to make the office better. I spent too much time on it, honestly. And that's because I couldn't figure out how to move the ball forward, even with the feedback. I was caring, hardworking, motivating, but were those the qualities that they needed? I've seen micromanagement, even did that early on, but moved away from it. I knew I didn't want to be like that kind of boss. But what I was doing was not working either. So why not? Did you know that only 30% of the workforce is engaged? That means 7 out of 10 people on your team are not engaged, according to Gallop. So what is causing such a massive disengagement? Well, we know that the biggest reason people leave their job is due to their manager. "People leave managers not companies...in the end, turnover is mostly a manager issue," Gallup wrote in its survey findings. The effect of poor management is widely felt. Gallup also determined that poorly managed work groups are on average 50 percent less productive and 44 percent less profitable than well-managed groups. So what is it then that us managers are not doing correctly?

The Top Traits of a Great Leader

Kouzes and Posner wrote one of the most authoritative works on leadership, called the Leadership Challenge. In it, they did a massive study spanning over 4 decades across the globe. They found that there are four most common and desired traits we want in a leader, that has proven the test of time, industry, and experience:

- Honesty. People trust leaders who are strong in their values/beliefs and show integrity in their actions.
- Forward Thinking. 71% want a leader with a vision. No one wants to follow someone that is lost.
- Competency. Someone that is capable of understanding the business and leading the team to success.
- Inspiration. Employees want someone who is energetic and positive, helping make the work more meaningful.

So the question becomes…how do you become this type of leader, if you are not this person right now? Is it possible to become this person? Some will say, "you just aren't cut out for leadership" or "you are the way you are and not likely to change." This is what I'll explain later as a fixed mindset. Your brain is actually quite capable and flexible of learning new habits and thinking patterns, proven by neuroscience. I'll also add, that leadership is a skill. It starts within, which is where most people fail to spend time in or recognize. Many use just outward, the power, the psychological-size, the influence, and that can be dangerous if not grounded in principles. Don't believe the lie, you can learn to be a great leader. Let's begin with a simple but powerful method that changed everything for me.

Utilize and Practice Daily Gratitude

You made the decision, you're doing this. You're in it to win it. Love It! If you have ever heard of emotional intelligence (EQ), it will now come into play for you in a massive way.

I remember hearing about EQ for the first time early in my leadership career. I had no idea what it was (red flag number one haha) but soon discovered that it's really important. EQ is two things: understanding and being aware of yourself and understanding and being aware of others – mainly their emotions, moods, and body language.

Don't overthink this. I did that at first, and it drove me nuts. EQ is a learned skill. You can learn it and grow it and get really really good at it over time and with practice. You are not a fixed asset. You are moldable, teachable, coachable, and capable of so much more. Remember that as we go through this.

You have natural instincts, reading the room, observing and noticing things. That's where this starts. A great way to practice emotional intelligence is to just go to a coffee shop, or a mall, or a restaurant, or any public place, and watch people interact for fifteen to twenty minutes. Literally, bring a note pad, find a place to sit, and people watch. Pick out five groups of people interacting with each other. Notice how they communicate with each other, and body language they use. What type of energy are they giving off? Do they seem happy, sad, mad, excited, anxious, distressed, hopeful, confident, tired, interested, not interested, eager, learning, checked out, supportive, caring, pissed off, frustrated? Isn't it interesting after reading those words that you can see in your mind what each of those people look like simply from body language, and not from what they're saying? Bingo. Do you think you can tell a lot about a person if you observed their behaviors, mood, and body language over several occurrences of observing them? Probably, and they would not have said a word.

Professor Mehrabian combined the statistical results of the two studies and came up with the now famous— and famously misused—rule that communication is only seven percent verbal and ninety-three percent non-verbal. The non-verbal component was made up of body language (fifty-five percent) and tone of voice (thirty-eight percent).

Body language and tonality, the way you say things, is more impactful than what you actually say. Now that you've done this exercise, think about these things when you're in conversations with people. Be interested, not interesting. (Secret sales tip.) Show interest and observe others, genuinely. You will learn so much, and you will be in tune emotionally with what's really going on.

The next step is yourself. Becoming self-aware. An easy place to start is just to be dead-honest with yourself. What are the reasons you were successful at something? What were the reasons you were not? If you judged yourself, you probably know most of the answer to these questions. The problem is that we want to be right more often than being accurate. We'll tell ourselves anything to feel good. You have to get used to being uncomfortable with yourself. It's a strange thing to say, but it's true. You have to be open to the idea that your perception could be off, that you're not really paying attention to what you are doing, and what's going around you. When you can start to self-diagnose, assess, implement changes, and see new results, it's a good sign you are becoming more self-aware. You are improving your EQ.

Successful CEOs and leaders have high EQs. They are aware of themselves and others. They are excellent at the emotional management of their team. When you can start your day noticing the moods and behaviors of your team in your office, you can start to see what's really going on with them. Forget the numbers, their production, that only tells part of the story. It's the tip of a gigantic iceberg. You need to know what's going on underneath the ice. That's where reality is really happening. That is a very vulnerable, secret, important, valuable place. That place is safeguarded with maximum security most advanced technological state of the art security systems, people's hearts, ambitions, and desires. You need trust to gain access to that. Unfortunately, it's too often that people's self-interest trumps whatever that person really needs, and they know it, and feel it, immediately. People can smell and see b.s. a mile away. In less than five seconds people can know if you are really listening to them or not. Do you want to be trusted? Be 100% genuinely interested in them, and quiet your thoughts. Put all the other million things you are worried about on a shelf somewhere else when you are engaged in a conversation with someone. None of it matters to that person, and that's all that matters, that person, spending their precious time and energy, with you.

But how in the world do you get better at this? What is a practical way to improve my EQ, my trust, and listening skills? I'm a very practical person. I like to have systems and solutions that work. I'm not the smartest person in the room, but with the right systems and processes, I can out result anyone.

The Most Important Thing in This Book, Seriously

So here we go, the mother of all things that you must learn from this book is G-R-A-T-I-T-U-D-E. It was Danelle Delgado, an incredible elite business strategist who taught me a most powerful lesson. Choose joy, always.

What does that mean? It means what it says. Choose joy in every single moment of your life. It may seem impossible. I get pissed off, frustrated, sad, mad, etc. at least once a day. Still, I choose joy. You're probably thinking right now, "But I'm not that type of person. You're naturally optimistic and a feel-good guy. I'm a realist, a pessimist, a whateverist." I don't care what you think you are. What you think you are is exactly why you are in this position right now. You need to change your thinking. Thinking creates behavior and mood, and that creates action and results, and consequences.

Here is your new code, your new blueprint, to start living today, forever. Do the following exercise one day, then a week, then a month, and then a year first. Forever will happen down the road.

Write down ten things you are grateful for when you wake up in the morning and ten things you are grateful for before you go to sleep. You need to buy a journal for this. I recommend the "I Choose Joy" journal by Danelle on Amazon (It's got some neat features in it that are captured in this book.). This is step one for practicing gratitude.

Step 2 is to implement your gratitude arsenal when you enter a hostile conversation, or thought, or feeling. You switch and pivot. You think about what you are grateful for, you choose joy, and whatever you are dealing with at the moment shall pass.

Have you seen the Pixar movie, Inside Out? It's such a great movie for kids and adults. It's about the five core emotions of people and how they get more complex as you grow older. You do not want to be Anger, the red-hot guy that shoots fire from his head when he goes off on something or someone. You want to be Joy, who always chooses joy.

But if you're like most of us, we tend to want to behave like Anger and just let it rip on someone or something when we feel fully justified to do so. It may feel good at the moment. I assure you it only leads to tears and hurt afterward.

Step 3 in practicing gratitude is to create your emotional reaction filter. You do not want a nuclear meltdown in your situation. You need to activate your self-awareness defense system and realize what is pissing you off, making you sad, or whatever emotion it's creating that is affecting your flow state. Acknowledge it. Have compassion toward it, and almost like you are giving it the bird choose joy instead, smile, and walk away.

Use Your Words Wisely

In Indiana Jones and the Last Crusade (If you haven't seen it, rent it. It's a classic of our lifetime), Indiana has to choose the right Holy Grail, and not the fakes, to save his father and ultimately escape the hidden cave he's in. Choose poorly, you die. Choose wisely, you live. It's a great metaphor.

Step 4. You must taste your words before you spit them out. Another powerful lesson I learned from my mentor. Will your words edify, support, lift up, help, encourage, motivate, love someone? Or will they tear them down? Are your words used to promote your own self-interest? Do they belittle, bully, depress, suppress, or demotivate someone? If it's the latter, please use your gratitude filter and not speak. Taste your words, and if they're good and coming from the right place, then speak away. They are gifts to the world and will create awesome moments and results. Your words are extremely powerful. They can literally create or destroy anything or anyone. Not to get to religious on you again, but that is literally what we know Genesis to be when God created the world. He spoke it into existence, and it was created. We are made in the image of our Creator. We have supernatural powers that are taken for granted every day, totally misused and undervalued.

If you do nothing else from this book but practice gratitude, be self-aware and be intentional with your words, you will move mountains in your life. I 100% guarantee that.

In summary:

- Get a journal
- Write ten things you are grateful for in the morning, and at night. (Write down your top goals for the day, too (Chapter 4))
- Use your gratitude filter defense system
- Choose your words wisely, and create your world and relationships

CHAPTER 6

Change Your Circles of Influence

Your Outside Forces Make a Huge Impact to Your Future

Ok, we just talked about controlling your thoughts and practicing gratitude. Now, we address the outside factors. Where, who, and what are you getting your daily information from? What are people telling you on a daily basis about you? Who is in your "war room" of your mind? Who gets to see what's under the iceberg? Who is allowed access to you?

Napoleon Hill in his book *Think and Grow Rich* talks about having a board of advisors for your life. Even, if they're dead. Yeah, he had in his board of advisors people like Abe Lincoln, Jefferson, and others, plus some of the greatest American Industry Icons like

Ford, Rockefeller, Morgan, etc. Does that sound crazy to you? It might and that's ok, but let's give this some fair perspective. Did you read about iconic figures in history growing up in school or outside school? Like Martin Luther King for example. So many people look at his courageous leadership as him fighting for what he 100% believed in with all his heart, for what the world needed and deserved. He had conviction to his core. Nothing could shake him, and no one would stop him. He had his Rubicon moment and never looked back. Living people now look back and learn from examples like him, and other passed heroes, all the time. You know what they stood for, you know their actions, you could imagine their counsel to you.

Massive success often results from collaboration. Putting multiple geniuses in a room together can do amazing things. That's what makes companies so successful and is why they grow. You hire and collaborate with beautiful minds and gifted talent that are all unique and different from you.

The five people you spend the most time within your life, right now, are where your potential lies. The average of those five people's income, wealth, ability, influence, character, and depth in development are where your ceiling is today. That's what my grandfather told my dad and me. I'll never forget it, and I've heard it from numerous ultra-successful entrepreneurs and business people. It's 100% true.

Don't believe me? When I changed who I allowed to influence me for the better just under two years ago, my knowledge grew exponentially.

Before:
- I hated reading and read one or two books a year, not to mention my income was flat for five years
- My influence was minimal
- I couldn't hold a team together if my life depended on it

After:
- I read over thirty books
- My income grew by 250%
- I spoke at multiple business conferences
- Appointed to two boards of directors
- I had no turnover in two years and everyone thrived to the highest performance in their career
- There is no mistake. These are not accidents. They are direct results from getting input and influence from the right places and people.

Who in your life right now is telling you that you can't? That you're not smart enough, not ready, not skilled enough, someone is better than you for that job, that goal is reserved for someone else, your dream or goal is unrealistic, unattainable, your business plans and goals are too far-reaching, you're not a good parent, you're not a good spouse. If someone gives you the "yeah right smile" or laughs at you in dismay or disbelief, or thinks you're crazy for whatever idea your genius came up with then get these people far away from you!

Maybe you can't though. Maybe it's your spouse, your best friend, your employer, or boss. Those are more tricky to solve in a moment. But at the very least, you need to seriously evaluate who you are allowing to influence your thoughts and decisions for your life.

You only have one life. This one. You're alive today, but today may be your last day. Sad to think, but true. Do you know someone that has cancer? Have you had friends and family members pass away unexpectedly or too soon? Yeah, it's not you today, but it could be. Do you want to have regret when it's all over? I sure as heck don't. Not when we're living in the most amazing and opportunity-filled country in modern history. You have limitless opportunities to be who you want to be, do what you want to do.

Try this for an exercise. You'll need that journal again.

Name the five people you spend the most time with right now. Then do the same thing but focus on certain parts of your life. This should give you a lot of self-awareness (EQ) as to what is going on in your life.

- Five people for your business growth and success
- Five people for your wealth building
- Five people for your professional development
- Five people for your health and wellness
- Five people for your family life
- Five people for your spiritual life

You just listed the top thirty influencers that you've allowed to affect your entire life right now. Look at the list. Do you like it? What don't you like? Are there stud number one draft picks out there that would game change any one of those categories? What about if you could create the All-Star five-person team for that category? Who would they be and why? What would you hope to learn from them? What would your life be like with your list resorted, revamped, with who you want on it?

This is your life, is it not? I tend to believe that I'm on borrowed time. My life is His and I want Him to do what He wants with it. But we were given freedom of choice. We were given (a gift) of choice. You can choose whatever and whoever you want in your life today.

What is worth more to you: achieving your dreams and your potential, or succumbing to the status quo so you don't hurt someone's feelings? Are you willing to spend less time with those people that won't support your dream? Are you willing to hard conversations and stand up for what you believe in at your core? Are you willing to defend and stand up for what you value?

One little trick I learned on my journey to now is that when something bothers me, causes a disruption in my flow, it usually means that it's something that doesn't agree with my values. Do you know what your values are? You have them, I guarantee it. If you need help figuring this out, be self-aware when you're in conversations and notice how they make you feel. What does that mean about what you care about?

I want you to write down your values below. What's your life mission statement, your business mission statement? What do you stand for? What do you care about? Why do you do what you do? What's the purpose in it?

Simon Sinek says that knowing your why is the most powerful thing to have clarity on in your business, and life. When you can structure your behaviors and actions around your why, the what, how, and who will come a lot more naturally.

Before you move forward in this book, please do this exercise for yourself. Take ten to fifteen minutes, to fill in the list below. It won't take long.

- Your mission:
- Your values:
- Your vision for the life you want to create:

- Your top five influencers in each category:

You may think that your influencers are not reachable, that they don't have time for you, that you'll never really get to meet or work with them. Stop it. We are living on the most connected planet of all time. Do you have an Instagram account? It will change one day, but for now, right now, you can direct message anyone in the world. And most influencers are not too busy to get back to you. Keep showing up and finding ways to connect to them. Give them reasons for wanting to work with you or help you. It may take months or even a couple of years, but you can find ways for these people to be in your life, if you really want it. Look at the people I mentioned I met in Chapter 2. I am doing projects and collaborations with multiple people on that list. I'm reaching up! Reach reach reach! Rise above the noise, above mediocrity, above the average of your life right now.

How to Get a Meeting with an Influencer

I'm going to share a killer secret with you. Please, please, please do not abuse this. Do it for the right reasons, and you will be blessed. Do not, and you will die. Just kidding but think Indiana Jones. Don't mess with karma man, it will backfire on you!

Here it is:

Do you have a LinkedIn account? Are you in any industry association for your business? Chamber of Commerce?

While your ultimate top five list may take time to reach, you can work toward it by meeting other influencers who are still worthy of being in maybe your next five, or top fifteen or twenty. Find who lives near you in your area. Who can you get access to the easiest? Not sure?

Here's an example:

Join an industry association that matches your business. Many business associations have directories of members on their website that you can download. This contains their phone or email usually. Call and email them and say something like this:

"Hi CEO XYZ,

I just joined the chapter for this association and noticed you're one of its leading members. I'm under the impression this chapter values mentorship, and that's what really drew me in to join. I'm an ambitious professional and want to learn more from people like you about how you became successful in your career. Would you be open to a conversation about that?"

Best, your name"

You know how many people said yes to that? Nearly 100%. I met with some of the most successful leaders and CEOs in my industry. They cleared their schedules (which is very hard to do), sat down with me, and willingly gave me their sage advice. Some even offered to do a long-term mentorship with me.

Thank them with your gratitude, send a thank you note. Keep in touch with them. Build your book of influencers. Update them with how you're doing. Do this month after month. You will be well on your way. Not to mention, the things you will learn, and things you already know deep down from your own intuition, are 100% going to happen.

You can do this! Are you excited right now? How do you feel compared to when you started this book? Write that down in your journal too. Along with your expressions of gratitude, I want you to jot down a couple quick takeaways each day from now on. You are starting to document your journey. I can't wait to see and hear your story someday.

If I don't earn the opportunity to work with you one on one, perhaps we can connect on business travels if I'm in a city near you. I would love to meet you and hear how you are doing!

Up next, hyper-growing your sales. Get ready to be a rainmaker.

BONUS GOODIES JUST FOR YOU!

Go to **www.jamesjacobi.com/goodies** for secret access to 4 pieces of training on:

1. Taking the First Step - Becoming the Leader Within
2. Know Your Value - How to Become the Expert Your Client Needs
3. Show Your Value - How to Outshine Your Competition
4. Force Your Win - How to Have Unshakable Confidence and Close Business

If you want more help, book a call with me now. Just visit **https://JamesJacobi.as.me/**

YOU CANNOT FIND THIS PAGE FROM MY WEBSITE. IT'S A SECRET BETWEEN YOU AND ME, HERE. IT'S WORTH THOUSANDS OF DOLLARS, BUT FOR YOU IT'S FREE. I WANT TO HELP YOU WIN, RIGHT NOW, WHERE YOU ARE AT. YOU'VE GOT THIS! :-)

CHAPTER 7

Catch Fire Your
Sales Growth

Grow Sales 400% in 90 Days

While it was amazing to most that I came back to
New Jersey and got our new line of business off the
ground and up to $1.3M RR in sales in ninety days,
which usually takes sales teams two years to do, that
was small for me. It really was. I had the mindset to do
the unforeseen and move mountains. And I've done that
type of growth dozens of times in the past. It wasn't new
to me, or beyond my grasp. And that's where I want to
start with you. The long-term goal here, and short too, is
to produce predictable results. But how do you do that
if you've never been to that summit of success? Great

question, we're going to go through some practical strategies of how to do this.

Mental Game

Good morning, good afternoon, good evening. You are not allowed to have negative thoughts. Wherever you're at, your new rule to live by is no negativity allowed. Think about what you think about for a second. (I'd actually recommend doing this daily as it's a form of meditation and very helpful.) What does a negative thought do to you? How does it affect your body, your emotions, your mood, your behaviors, your results? It brings you down, shuts you down. You feel like crap physically. Your clarity is out the window. Your energy can be felt across the room. Your teammates and customers see and feel it without you saying a word

Does gratitude grow sales? Yes, it does. People want to do business with people they know, like, and trust. You're much more likable if you're in a good mood. People get supercharged off your energy. You're refreshing to be around. They want more of whatever you've got cooking in your mental kitchen. It helps your confidence and your self-worth. Confidence is very attractive to people. But what happens when you are not confident? I've been there, for years at a time. When you are struggling and are not seeing many wins and tons of losses, it feels impossible to be confident and in a good mood. And as you may know, the mood is so important for your team to see. It sets the tone for the office and the day. What is the mood that you bring into the office each day?

Do not fake it until you make it. That's a weak strategy. People can see authenticity and integrity. You can't hide it, so don't even try.

Rather, make a choice. Remember, you have to choose your thoughts and pivot, many times a day, from the negativity tape of yesterday that plays in your head. Yesterday is gone, and it's never coming back. You were given the gift of today to live. Tomorrow is promised to no one. Be grateful for that and appreciate YOU. You are an interesting, fantastic, genius, successful human being. That's your baseline, nothing else. Now it's your job to choose thoughts and actions that reflect that for the rest of your day today. You just have to focus on today, don't worry about tomorrow.

Affirmations

Here is a very powerful strategy to get you in alignment and in the right mental place to freaking crush it. Affirmations are simply short statements about yourself. They hold claim to your identity, your life goals, your vision, your truth. You can have as many or as few as you want, but the exercise I want you to do to now is write down three affirmations on an index card, or in your journal, that you can look at throughout your day today. Here's are some examples:

I am the most successful salesperson in the world

I am the most self-aware leader ever known

I am a leader of strong values and conviction

I am a leader that runs a $100M business (future state, claiming it today)

I have had more promotions on my team than anyone in the history of the company

I hire qualified, highly skilled, and courageous geniuses on my team

I am the master of all to closing a deal

I am the most admired and desired business for my customer in the marketplace

> *"Whether you think you can, or can't, you're right."*
> **–HENRY FORD**

I wrote down on my vision board that I would create and grow a $50M business and team by 2020 (a three to five year window). That's a target and a vision I can claim as truth.

When you set your targets high, 100x high, your thinking and problem-solving genius changes trajectory. Do you want to figure out how to run a $100M business or a $1M business? What kind of customers and sales volume, how many orders, how many meetings, how many calls, how many closes, how many contracts would you need to achieve to hit that goal?

Map It Out

Remember, write down one day, one week, one month, one-year goals. Work backward and break it down by what you will need to do. You might be thinking that you've done this before and that you've done these processes or deals hundreds or thousands of times over, and that it is impossible given the timeframe. Or that it would require significantly more staff and you don't have the time or money to hire that size right now. If this is what you're thinking, I'm glad you see the flaws in the plan. That just means you change the plan, not the result. The result is possible my friend, you just have to look at different angles.

Leverage and Momentum Are King and Queen to Scaling Fast

Think about physics for a second. Which one gets more distance? An arrow from a bow, or a bullet from a gun? What about a wind-up toy race car? If you wind it up a couple times, versus ten times, which one goes further, faster, and longer? You have to create leverage, and momentum in your sales growth to go faster, higher, and longer.

But how the heck do you do that? Simple, you have a few options:

Get clients that buy in bulk, many times over, versus one-off orders from a client. This alone catapult your sales.

Raise your prices, significantly. Would that turn people away? Yeah, probably. You would turn away the customers that are killing your business right now. That's a good thing. You want customers that would skyrocket your business. You might be thinking that no one can charge that high in a marketplace and get away with it. To that, I say look at the clothes you buy, the restaurants where you eat, the cars you buy, the home you live in, the technology solutions and software you buy, the rent you pay for commercial real estate, your mortgage on your house, capital equipment for business, etc. There are for sure low quality and low-price options, but there are also high quality and high price options in every category. Which are you for your business? You need to pick one, but don't be both. You'll confuse potential customers and it will be very hard for you to scale. You can still scale with low price, low quality by the way. That might be your jam. Look at Walmart. They're the largest company in the world, and they sell things at the lowest possible price. Their leverage points are not revenue from high prices, but the mass volume of sales in bulk at low prices plus supply chain mastery with very efficient operating costs.

You have to decide what makes sense for you and what your competitive strengths and advantages are. I have more experience in the high quality, high-value space, so that is the perspective I refer to as I write this. But you can apply this to the opposite.

With that said, let's look at finding clients that make the most sense for your business goals and plan.

Your Ideal Customer

Who are they? What do they care about? What problems are they trying to solve in their business? What's their competitive advantage over their competition, and what are their weaknesses? Just as if you were to go to war, you better know as the Commander in Chief what you're up against. How does your opponent think, act, behave? What's their routine in the business calendar of the year? Do they have seasonal spikes of buys or triggers in their business that occur like clockwork on an annual basis? These are all things you need to learn and understand to position yourself in the right place and the right time for you to be the hero.

Then you need to understand the people within the organization. Who are the leaders? What do they care about in and outside of work? What are their values and vision for why they do what they do? How do they buy from services or products like you? What's been their experience with a competitor to you? What features or benefits are important, and not important, to what your product or service offers?

All this requires market study and surveillance. You need to know the marketplace for your product or service better than anyone. How many competing organizations that you know of ask their salesforce to go and get meetings and get new accounts? All of them. As many as you can, they say. They just point to a number weekly and say, "Hit that number, go!" And on a daily and weekly basis, they push their sales staff to go out in a frenzy and conjure up business, with little to no direction, strategy or method that would yield the type of results they really want. You want predictable, repeatable massive sales growth for every person on your team, right? If so, here is my first sales strategy:

Slow down to move faster. If you cannot provide answers to all the questions I just laid out above, then do not expect quality sales meetings and high sales volume. Just don't go there. Instead, for you and your team, do the following:

Interview Your Market

Interview your prospective clients before you sell them anything. Your number one goal for customer acquisition and growth should be, how can I best serve my clients so they achieve their strategic annual goals, better than anyone else could? That's it. You have the correct answer and ability to repeat that result. You win.

Try using scripts and reach-outs like this with your prospective clients:

On LinkedIn, connect with five people in the organization if they're small, ten to twenty if they're midsize (50M - 500M), and twenty-five to fifty if they're over 500M+. Don't just add them either, that's a rookie move Use a simple but effective message like this:

> *"Hi John,*
> *I saw you are xyz position at abc company. I am also a leader in that industry and am curious to learn from experts like yourself. Would you be open to a conversation? I have a breakthrough proof of concept I'm developing and need feedback from market leaders like yourself. It's just a few questions and I only need five minutes.*
>
> *Best, James"*

Something like that. People like to help people. People like to get their ego stroked. People like to be interested and intrigued by something. Create messaging that does all those things, and then ask questions as I mentioned above to get valuable feedback that can help you understand what the market really needs, and the blueprint for how you can freaking crush it and be their hero.

Build whatever they're telling you. Don't build what you think is cool but have zero market validation on. If your customer is telling you they will buy in bulk, all day every day if you can do XYZ, then by God go do that if you can. Build that solution for them before someone else does. They're shopping for it. Unfortunately, I too often see companies shoving products or services down customers' throats when they don't even know if it's what they really want. It's a terrible strategy and doomed to disappoint. You are in the business of solving problems, period. If your business doesn't solve a problem really well, it will not grow or perform the way you want it to. You'll have to change your business model and fast.

To summarize, you need to know your customer and marketplace better than anyone. Then you build the perfect solution to solve their problem. Then, you will truly know your value for whom you serve. And it's the best possible solution they've ever seen. And this makes you extremely confident in persuading and selling this to your ideal customer, because you know for sure it will help them. How much more fun is that?

How Much You Charge

This is completely up to you. I will tell you that higher prices and higher margins, will skyrocket your total sales volume alongside the bulk buys you're getting. Is your price worth it? Darn straight it is. You will overdeliver more than your customer has ever experienced. You do have the best product or solution, don't you? Then DO NOT shrink on price objections. You are worth every penny. Not to mention, higher price triggers in the mind a higher quality of service and expectation anyway. Which is what you are (if that's your strategy). In my case, it was. I was the expert in my marketplace, and could out know, out-will, out-last, out-sell, out deliver anyone else you could put against me. I was 1,000% confident in that. So, you know what my time and effort are worth, to provide that much value to my customer? A heck of a lot more than the average and mediocre marketplace of my industry competition. Peers and competitor friends of mine couldn't believe how much I was charging and how much business I was getting. It wasn't even close to their numbers. I made sure, no matter what, that we always, always, always did right by our client. They will say without prompting that we were worth every penny. And that mindset and service level are what you need to win big. Do whatever it takes to make your clients win. When they win, you win. They will promote you 'til the end of time. This is how you scale organically and fast.

Show Your Value

Now that you've wound up your energy by going slow and studying your next moves (just like chess), you can execute extremely fast. You can confidently show your value as much as possible and as fast as possible to your marketplace. I love what Grant Cardone teaches about this. He calls it "getting attention." If you are not being noticed or getting attention in the marketplace, it does not matter how good your service or product, no one will buy it because they don't know you exist. In his book *Sell or Be Sold*, the main theme is being completely and unconditionally sold on you, your product, and company. You have to be certain in every encounter you have with an individual. Confidence and certainty will win over in each conversation. If you don't feel certain, even though you know that you are superior in every way, then go back and use the affirmation process before your sales encounter. Pull out your card and read it right before you go into your meeting. Bring your mental A game, and then confidently show your value to the prospect.

You need to go from being unnoticed to completely dominating the market with attention. Advertise, promote, meet as many people as possible, share, and shout your solution to the world. Use every possible medium to get your message across. Yes, you'll have to build out a strategy for each and how you will effectively use your resources and time to do so, but you must build some type of plan with this. I'm talking about doing the following with some general guidelines:

LinkedIn - post three times per week (Mon, Wed, Fri)
Twitter - post five to fifteen times per day
Instagram - post daily
Facebook - post daily
YouTube - post one to two times per week
Podcast
Print media
Radio
Google AdWords
Networking events
Industry Association events
Chamber of Commerce
Email
Voicemail
Referrals

You need to slow down again and write out a one-page strategy for each medium. What do you want to do on it, how will you execute it, and how will you measure the results you're getting? What are your Key

Performance Indicators (KPIs) with all these types of marketing?

There are a lot of resources out there and consultants that can streamline this for you. You will be naturally better at some than others, but your target market exists on all of them in some form or another. You want to be noticed and get attention in the most cost-effective and scalable way possible. Build the system, map it out, then execute.

Ninety-Day Runs

Take your annual goals, your revenue goals, your 100x goals, and map out to complete them in ninety days. Make it consequential, meaning that if you do not achieve "x" in ninety days, then you have to do "y." What would happen if you hyper-focused for ninety days on your business? If you did all the right actions to create your results, what would that mean for you? What are you willing to give up for ninety days to go all in on this and make this happen? Put a massive reward for yourself and your team at the end of it. I'm not talking about hitting your sales quota from corporate, that's normal. I'm talking about 400% growth, supernatural, freakishly insane growth that will leave people dumbfounded. You need to plan your work and work your plan. Block out the world and just be relentless. Tim Grover talks a lot about this in his book *Relentless*. He's a high-performance coach, literally. He was *the* trainer for Michael Jordan, Kobe Bryant, Dwayne Wade, and others. If you really, really want the result you're aiming for, you have to be relentless, and a "cleaner" as he describes it. Simply put, no excuses and zero distractions. He gives a lot of examples of how Michael and Kobe would perform in a game, and how they would train and practice when there wasn't a game. It was 24/7 relentless focus and effort. There were no off days, there were no light practices. They went hard all the time. And when their bodies broke down, they called in Tim. He would fix them up mentally and physically, and then they went back out for more. There was only one goal, win the championship. We don't stop until the mission is accomplished. If you really want massive results, it requires massive action, sacrifice, giving up something else to gain what you want. Not everyone is cut out for it, or willing to do it. You have to be willing to do what others won't do.

Try this now: Schedule out your next ninety days. One of the common mistakes I see people make is they say, "I will work so hard and I will hit my goal! It will happen!" That's not enough to get you there. As GC says, one of the biggest mistakes people make is underestimating how long or how much effort it will take to achieve the massive goal you want. You need to build in a failure, unexpected detours, derailments, getting sick, family emergencies, into your plan. If they don't happen, fantastic! But you have to plan for them to happen, and then have your workable plan to still achieve your goal nonetheless. One way to start out your ninety-day plan is to first start out with your seven-day run. Set the tone, take ridiculous massive action, and see where that gets you and how far the needle moves. Then do it again for another seven days. Then another. Most people rationalize their little wins and slow down or give up. Don't take your foot off the gas, push down harder. You don't celebrate until the mission is done, complete.

Seven-Day Runs

Do everything I just said and do it in seven days. Impossible? Nope, negative thinking! One of the most overlooked but most powerful strategies you have at your arsenal, that everyone has, is your ability to condense time. Compress the time in which it takes you to get in front of a customer, close a deal, market your services. Leverage points. Which leverage points yield the highest ROI?

I'll give you an example: I had a big deal in the works, the biggest ever, actually, of my career. I did everything I mentioned above. We had several meetings, but that was over the course of four months. It wasn't closing, and time can kill your deal. My mentor challenged me to make $10,000 in a week. I had never done that before in my life. There are a lot of ways to actually do that, the one key ingredient being "action." You must take massive action to make the world move in your favor. Action means going out and reaching, connecting, and ensuring you make progress. It is not thinking or analyzing, those are the reasons most miss their window of opportunity.

I did something that I never had done before. I let my genius go to work and problem solve this for me. How could I secure $10,000 from this client in the next seven days, especially if we never bill until services are rendered? First, I made a extraodinary proposal. How did I know it was extraordinary? Well, first I looked at all the other proposals that I or someone else made that didn't work and didn't win business. I looked for common patterns that may shed light as to why. I asked myself the question again, what does my prospect care about in relation to the value I can provide, and what do they want to see on paper that would make it an easy "yes" to get started? I took out of the fluff about how great we are. I comprised my proposal for the following:

- My understanding of their problem (showing that I listened and understood them) and what solution they were looking for
- Social proof that we solved problems with other clients near exactly to what they were facing

- Financials and numbers showing comparison costs if they did or didn't do the deal
- ROI if they worked with us
- More social proof with written letters, cell phone numbers, and emails of people in roles at companies similar to theirs
- The ask and close: I gave them seven days to commit with a $10,000 retainer or we had to walk away. Other clients were knocking on our door and we knew that the type of service level they would require would mean we would have to forego other business to serve them well.

This was during the week of 4th of July and no one was at work. Most had taken Friday off at least. I left Kinkos on Thursday night and the next morning traveled into NYC to drop the proposals off. No one but a few was there at the business. I knew someone in the organization that worked in the key department I was working with on the deal, and she let me through security. She willingly placed all proposals on each stakeholder's desk, so they'd see it on Monday morning. Monday morning came, two hours into the morning, my phone rang.

"Hey, this is ABC person, my VP told me to call you, we need to figure out how to get this deal signed this week and work with you. I will be in touch"

Boom. It worked, touchdown!

I condensed time. I forced my win. You need to force your win, change, and move the world to your favor. There is absolutely nothing wrong with you persisting to the world that you need to get this done and get it done now. You do, in fact, have the best solution that can provide the most help, don't you? Then there is no time to waste. You must ACT NOW.

I used this same strategy again months later with five more companies I wanted to work with. I met a representative from each of the organizations and disseminated my proposal to the executive teams. We had conversations and got things moving.

Two Key Factors in Closing Your Deals

There are two ingredients to closing your clients as fast as possible.

Find and build a relationship that turns into them your champion. If you get someone inside the client with enough clout to tout your name to the decision makers that will listen, you will cut your sales cycle by 50% or more. I leverage networking and industry associations for this reason. You can still close deals via calls, emails, and meetings. But I found that leveraging a relationship from a networking event which catapulted me in front of the rest of the key decision makers in a very short amount of time.

Ask for the close and create urgency/scarcity. It is true that you cannot serve everyone in the marketplace right now. You do not have the bandwidth or the resources. So, give them a time limit, no more than five business days to make a decision. You have to move on and get other deals if they're not ready or not the right client. Create a consequence with it. If they really need you and want you, and you show that you want to help but you have to move on soon, they will react. They will tell you to wait, or they will buy right then and there.

The Last and Most Important Thing on Sales

As Gary Vee says, the number one marketing strategy in the world is C-A-R-E. The end.

He's right. I used to sell totally wrong and missed the boat completely. Do you want transactional buys and customers that have no loyalty? Or do you want life-long customers that will buy from you and promote you forever? You can have the second, but it requires a different game to play. You can't just sell your stuff, be kind, do a great job, and that's it. That's all important. But if you want your customer to really want to keep you around, you build loyalty from them. You become their trusted advisor. How do you do this? Serve with gratitude.

Yep, we're going there. This is why you are doing gratitudes in your daily routine. They apply 100% here to your sales strategy. Serve your clients first, before you sell and offer them anything. Think of it this way: When you meet someone for the first time, and shake their hand and say, "nice to meet you," do you have your other hand reaching into their pocket trying to take their money? Of course not, who would do that? Well, that's what you're doing if you meet someone and just ask for their money. Unfortunately, that's what most salespeople do, and that's why they suck and give sales a bad name.

How do you serve? Easy. Remember before when you did all that homework on your market, your customers, their people? Go even deeper. Find out about their hobbies, their family, what's important to them outside of work. What skill or industry segment are they interested to learn about to improve their results at work (that may have nothing to do with your product or service)? Here are some suggestions:

- Send them periodic articles that are relevant to their industry, saying you were thinking of them
- Send a short-hand written note saying you were thinking of them or asking them out to a fun event
- Send them an inexpensive gift, like a book or an iTunes card that they would enjoy
- Take them out to dinner

- Give them free information that educates them about your industry.
- Teach them how to buy from you, what to look for in your competitors that would add value to them
- Share insights you've found out from a conference you go to

Just do thoughtful, non-self-serving things. Do them from a place of gratitude and service. Give free and valuable information three to five times before you pitch and sell. Give before you take. Give more first. Learn to be generous.

When you service your clients, on the phone, in an email, or in person, have a gratitude mindset while you do it. I tell my clients all the time how grateful I am to work with them and that I appreciate their time and attention. I mean it 100% of the time. I am lucky to get their time and attention. EQ is applicable here.

Show your customer gratitude, teach them gratitude, show your team gratitude, teach your team gratitude. Lead from the front both with your customer and your team. What you are teaching and demonstrating will radically transform your relationships and interactions over time. I write down in my gratitude daily that I am grateful for the opportunity to work with my clients and my team. It's embedded in my subconscious. Care, do the right thing and do what you say you're going to do. Show gratitude. You will be unstoppable.

CHAPTER 8

Elevate Your Personal Brand

Become the Authority in Your Space

After obtaining a large client in New Jersey and servicing them for several months, the word got out. We were crushing it and people were noticing. I went to a networking event for small businesses in the community and talked with a local company that does social work services. I met the director and we had a great conversation. She was interested in bringing us into her company for a meeting with her executives, as she had a problem with staff and hiring that I could solve. Before the meeting took place, you know what she did? Yep, she checked with the clients I mentioned I worked with and verified my credibility and results. Your company's brand lives within yours. They go together but are separate. People in the marketplace knew of my company because they knew of me providing exceptional service to them. My company could have a great reputation, but if I am also not relevant and have an authority brand in the marketplace, then it is more challenging to get referrals and business. We ended up getting the business.

Get everything you can to validate and promote your personal brand. Get videos and written testimonials from your clients, email introductions to new prospects, reference client calls, and anything else you can think of. Your personal brand and reputation are huge for growing your business.

I was 32 and applying for my first board position. I was one of the only males, and about 20 years younger than everyone else on the board. Due to my personal brand with others, I had several executives vouch for me and give their recommendation. I became the first non-clinician board member of this chapter in their 25-year chapter history. When you think no one is paying attention or looking, they are. All the times you don't know what value you are getting for yourself by serving others genuinely first, it's this. You are building your brand, and your brand will pay dividends sooner than later.

A personal brand is something that seems to have caught fire in the last few years. I know Gary Vee and others started talking about it almost ten years ago, but it's taken a while to catch on. And honestly, it still has plenty of time to. For those who take advantage right now of building your personal brand, you are doing the most valuable thing you can possibly do for sake of yourself and your family. Outside whatever long-term wealth strategy you have for retirement, this would be just as important if not more important than that.

I've had an interesting journey to my personal brand, to say the least. I will share some of the details of that journey here, and also some expert advice from one of my influencers, Gary Vee:

If your company does not allow you to build your own brand outside of the company, and if they won't let you build on a passion outside work hours, get out. I'm not telling you to become an entrepreneur, but maybe! What I am telling you to do is do what you are happy and excited about. Find a way to build and integrate that into your life. Do not do something for thirty to forty years just to make money. You are living in the most opportunity-filled era ever in our nation's history to do what you love and make money at the same time.

As Gary Vee says: "Any company that clamps down on its best talent and doesn't allow them to talk to the public is holding that talent back from where the business world is going and you don't want to be left behind. Without the freedom to develop a personal brand, you will find yourself at a strong disadvantage to the Competition."

Your personal brand is everything. I do not care what anyone else says differently on this. I will strongly disagree with them.

What happens if you lose your job, and you were not allowed to build your brand in and outside work? Who would know you? Who would know anything about you, what your value is, or what you could bring to the market? Nobody. Slap on a non-compete and you are in a pretty tough spot to find meaningful and skilled work that pays the bills.

I started learning about a personal brand when I hired my mentor from Grant Cardone's 10x conference. She taught me and my wife how to view ourselves differently. And it's not a crazy concept, but it's simply this:

You are unique, highly valuable, an asset, and a game-changer to help someone that needs it. You have skills and personal IP (intellectual property) that no one else has. You can offer someone something of value. You can build influence from who you are and what you care about. You can build influence on what you know and educate others. You can monetize your skills and your brand.

As I write this, I am in transition from my corporate life to serving you all with this book and offering future services to help you. I posted on LinkedIn and Facebook that I was now available in the job market. Guess how many responses I got on the first day? About sixty. Most with leads or direct access to jobs that were not posted. There were many who personally introduced me and connected me straight to a hiring leader, and I went on to interviews immediately. I did not have to apply, nor did I get any response from a job post. That is the power of personal brand. When you serve people unselfishly, just to do the right thing, for years on end, they never forget that. You never asked for a return favor and didn't have to. People want to help me because they respect me and want the best for me. I cared about them first, and they care about me in return.

What is your personal brand? As my brand grew, I got to do a live podcast at my former employer that was shared internally to everyone. It was the first time the conversation was being talked about. It was exciting and awesome. People were also scared and nervous though. Don't be scared or nervous. A personal brand is YOU. That's it. It is who you are, how you show up every day, what you show and represent to the people around you and to the marketplace. It's how you interact at networking events. It's what you post on social media. (Please post on social media if you can!) It's what you stand for. It's your mission, your vision, and your values for your life. It's your wonderfully and fearfully made unique gifts that were meant to be shared with the world. You have a brand that is meant to serve others. I can't put it more simply than that.

You have one life, one opportunity, one at-bat. You get to be and do you and show the world. Do not care what people think about you, please. I struggled with it too long in my life. Do you know what and where that got me? Nothing and nowhere. It added no value to shrink and try to be shards of myself or try to be someone else. You do not have to be anyone else, but you. You are more than enough to achieve the dreams you have.

Here's a secret: People don't think about you for you. People think about themselves and compare you to their own insecurities. You are a reflection of their own insecurities. Try this idea out on yourself. Look in the mirror.

Tim Grover says, "The problem when you look in the mirror, is not what you do see, but what you don't." Meaning, do you actually see the glorious and amazing human being you are when you look in the mirror? Or do you judge yourself and put yourself down immediately about something? Most of us do the latter. Our brains have been wired from wrong thinking. We've been influenced by the wrong influencers in society.

During my mentorship that helped me come to grips with who I am, there was a group of us in the mastermind that had the opportunity to go to Bora Bora. Yes, I said Bora Bora. What a beautiful and amazing place! Yeah, we maxed out our credit cards to go. We did everything sensibly wrong that you shouldn't do with your finances. But this trip was not meant to be an exotic trip. It was much more than that. It was a trip that signified we were burning the boats. We were leaving behind the old thinking and the old lifestyle that didn't serve us well. Our old ways were not helping us reach our goals, our life goals, our financial goals, our relationship goals, our influencer and learning goals, our faith goals. This move was to go all in, spiritually, financially, emotionally and physically.

When you 100% bet on you, the ROI is massive. I made all our money back and then some. I made more in the next six months than I had in the last two years. I became a better version of myself. I decided that no matter what, I would be me, and not care what others thought.

That led me to be on stage to speak for the first time and influence hundreds of business professionals with my story and shared learnings that could help their business grow. That lead to me going to Forbes, and L.A., to meet all those billionaires and brilliant minds, etc. That led to me to being appointed to boards. I was 100% authentically me, proud of it, and wanted to show the world so I could serve and help in any way I could.

Authority Marketing

Justin Blatt who works for ForbesBooks wrote a book on this, and I met him at the Forbes launch party. He makes a great point, and that is you can be wildly successful with your business and your life, if your marketplace where you serve knows you as the ultimate authority on your subject matter. Hence, your brand. This is posting your own articles on LinkedIn or blogs, videos on Facebook and YouTube, editorials in publications, etc. You have to push and reach and push to get your name out there. But when people know about you, they know what to expect and who you are when they meet you. You are seeding your marketplace to prosper with your services and value you offer.

Build in time to grow your personal brand. It is leadership, it is showing your team that everyone's uniqueness matters. Encourage them to grow theirs too. The more people know who you are, the more your business has a chance of being noticed in the marketplace. Your brand 100% and unequivocally helps your company brand. Period, stop.

Build your brand, connect with as many people as you can on social media and in person, and have a blast doing it. Build quality relationships. Serve, and you win.

CHAPTER 9

Serve Your People with Radical Integrity

The Blueprint to Building Your Tribe

You can do nothing without your team. Your team is crucial for everything from scaling your business to hitting your goals. Serve them and lead them well, you win. Don't, and you lose.

I was a terrible manager when I first became one. I had no idea what I was doing. I made tons of mistakes, many times over, and saw way more failures than wins. Turning over your team is not fun, and I did it about three times. I'm guilty as charged. It was me. I didn't want to admit it then, but it totally was. I had the best intentions too, really. But incompetence and lack of skill will hurt your people. But it's more than that. Without the right foundation everywhere else in your life, you cannot expect to have magical results with your team. You have to have integrity with your whole being and life. You need congruence. You need to be the same person in and outside work, not different. How can you have alter-egos? Many do and look at what happens. They drink too much. They have sex outside of their marriages, gamble, overeat, gain tons of weight, have wild mood swings in the office and at home, they get depressed, and have mental health issues. I thought that I had to have it all together around my people, that I had to hide my inner battles, put on a show, and have this gregarious confidence type look. Have you ever felt like you had to be someone else, act like someone else to be cool? Yeah, that's what I was doing. I thought I had to act like other leaders I know, but I was neglecting who I was. And because I was doing that, I was setting an example for my staff to do the same. Everything was shallow, and it is tough to build a bought-in team around that. I never felt secure with my team. I was always afraid of losing someone, not being good enough, etc. (Do you see how this weak mindset created the results?)

One of the saddest moments of my career was finding out that my twenty-six-year-old staff member who I managed and locked arms with every day, overdosed on heroin and passed away. I knew that massive student debt loans and other things were stressing him out a lot. I was a very imperfect sales director at the time, but I tried my best to support him and help him become great. He hit his all-time high numbers just before he decided our line of work was not for him anymore. He was tribe though, ride or die. He was not your typical salesperson. He had his quirks as we all do, but his heart was so awesome. I loved the guy. He gave everything he had to win, serve, and help his team. He never gave up. He persisted until he hit his mountain top. I cried so hard when I learned of his passing.

Business relationships are real people, life outside work is just as, if not more, important than work. I wish I could be the person I am today to travel back in time to be a better influencer to him, maybe it would have helped, maybe it wouldn't. You need mechanisms, defense systems, the correct influencers in your life, to keep your life sane, happy, and moving in the right direction. Having a growth mindset is everything, versus a fixed mindset.

I bring this story up, too, because we all have reasons for why we're at work. We must know and understand those. It's a big part of what's underneath that ice, knowing we need to be responsible and careful as their leader.

What was the difference between then and now? How did I build a highly performing tribe who were totally committed and never quit? I used the tools I lay out here:

Be totally authentic in demeanor and message

Serve your team with radical integrity

Show vulnerability to your iceberg reveals other's they can do the same

Have a growth mindset to yourself, then your team, creates a safe place for everyone's genius

Set your team up for success as it makes execution and growth a lot easier

Recognize and praise your team often, and record it

Be Totally Authentic

You hear that a lot these days, "be authentic." What does that mean? It's really simple actually. It means just be yourself. Do not try to act or be someone else. Your uniqueness is actually the best thing about you and the strongest part of your personal brand. It's what separates you from anyone else. Yet, we have the tendency to think small and be like others. This is exactly what I did first, and it didn't work. You can't expect someone to trust you if you are not confident in your own skin.

You cannot care about what others think of you. This was one of the hardest things I had to learn early in leadership. I cared way too much what my executive team and peers thought of me, and then also my staff. Leadership is not a popularity contest or being liked. And you're probably going to say it's about being respected. Well, yes and no. I actually think it should and can be both. People think respected means they have to strike fear into people and be tough. There's a time for being strong and firm, but it's not all the time. To be respected is not easy, you cannot care what people above you and below you (organizationally speaking) think of you. You have to make your decisions and your voice has to be the most confident and strongest. You 100% will make bad decisions and mistakes. It's life!!! That is totally normal. Your team is better off seeing you make mistakes, and watching you have a sense of humor about it, learning from it, and then implementing strategies to improve. That will teach them how to respond to their own mistakes.

On the other hand, PsychologyToday.com says that if behind what a person says and does is a defensive and self-deceptive approach to life, then no matter how passionate and committed they are to a cause, ultimately they are not being true to themselves. Authenticity is ultimately about those qualities that show healthy non-defensive functioning and psychological maturity. Those are the qualities we need to look for.

Serving Your Team with Vulnerability and Radical Integrity

Here's the big boy stuff. What you say, how you carry yourself, what you follow through on, is huge for your team. You need to have radical integrity. Here's what it looks like and how to live it:

Set a vision with your team for who you all want to be, where you want to go, and how you will get there.

It's time to implement your gratitude rituals, affirmations, and EQ strategies with your team. You must teach them how to do this. Personal and professional development is a non-negotiable if they are going to be working for you. No exceptions. I want people on my team who want to learn, get better, are hungry for success, willing to work the hardest they ever have, want to have fun, want to achieve something so massively great together, willing to share their genius with me, and I with them. This is the type of team that will help you grow 400% in 90 days, and much more beyond that. This is the team that will never leave you. I implemented this approach and strategies, we had zero turnover. I used to worry all the time if my team and I were in sync, if I'm leading the right way, if we're going to make it, how to prevent them from quitting. All that...gone with this. I never had to worry once. I knew to my core that our team was tight, and we would move mountains together. All I had to do was lead with radical integrity and be me. Be 100% authentic so they could be 100% authentic. Business is so much more fun this way!

I'll share with you some of the things I did to get this approach integrated. As I learned new things on how to be better, I shared and taught them to my team. I bought them all journals and asked them to do gratitude with me. We had weekly evening zoom calls and did mentorship and personal development training, and sales training. We had awesome conversations that we just didn't have time to do at work.

This was building a tribe. I learned what this meant after I read Seth Godin's book, Tribes. I highly recommend it. It's freaking awesome on how to be authentically leading and building an organic tribe. A tribe that has values, mission, and vision. A tribe that fights and cheers in unison. A tribe that will do anything for each other. Our values were excellence, bring and deliver results no matter what, have fun and not get too serious, direct honesty and vulnerability, and never giving up. We did it. We freaking crushed it. We had hockey stick growth, we loved serving our clients, and we had fun learning and growing together.

Was it all sunshine and rainbows? No. We had tons of valleys and challenges to overcome. But we overcame them, all of them. We found a way every time, and we did it together. We trusted and knew what our roles were, and we gave each other space to do our jobs. Which leads to my next point.

Have a Growth Mindset

Mindset by Carol Dweck explains the difference between a growth and a fixed mindset. A fixed mindset says: You are who you are, you can't change. This means that if you aren't good at something, you probably never will be. And this is the mindset and false truth I accepted about my management and leadership ability. I sucked so, therefore, I must suck and not be cut out for leadership. I had low EQ at first, unaware and oblivious to moods and emotions, which must have meant that I was subhuman and couldn't form great relationships. The self-talk of a fixed mindset is toxic and will tear down your dream. It holds you back from who you really are.

A growth mindset says, I may not understand what I'm doing now, but I can learn and get better. I may currently struggle with this task, but I can and will get to my goal by getting better every day. It's a getting-better-every-day mentality. It's progress. You can make progress, and move the needle, through effort, self-reflection, adjustment, and trying again. It's also owning 100% of your results, bad or good. If you suck and messed up, the growth mindset says "I know I sucked. I messed up. I want to get better and learn, and I'll get better every day. What could have I done better there? I'll adjust for next time." A growth mindset says that it is scientifically proven that you can rewire and change your thinking and brain cells. You can literally change how you behave and think over time.

When I met all those wildly successful people I mentioned earlier, the number one thing they all said that was the key factor for their success, was changing their mindset. Having a growth mindset.

For learning more about growth mindset strategies, I highly recommend checking out Tom Bilyeu's Facebook and Instagram pages, which can be found at @ImpactTheory.

A growth mindset is critically important because it shapes how you engage your team. It changes how you view and look at what they're doing and what performance stands for. There is no judgment on your team with a growth mindset. Your job is to help them learn, grow, and get better every day. You must create an environment where they feel safe with you.

Show Vulnerability to Your Iceberg, so You Can Empower Other's to Do the Same

Show your team that you are not perfect, that you are getting better every day, that you are vulnerable too. Show what's underneath your iceberg. It's the only way they'll show you theirs. According to the U.S. Department of Homeland Security, 7/8ths of an iceberg is below the water line. Just like an iceberg, we show very little of ourselves at work and in our relationships, at first. Under the iceberg, you see the pain, discipline, motivation, reasons, fears, ideas, genius creativity, late nights, conversations with your family and peers about work, the thousand thoughts about work outside of work. Yet, we only measure what's on the surface and dare to project what it means and its value. If you understood more of what's beneath, you'd be able to maximize, optimize, project, and foresee where that iceberg is going. It's the same with your team. You need to get to know them, how they think, what they think, and why they think it. You have to show them your iceberg first and create a safe space. This is no different than "sales." You are providing value and selling safety by showing them first how to do it and what it looks like. You must have and build trust in your team. You need to make it so they feel safe to try new things, create and share ideas, mess up and get back up, space to learn, play and grow.

Set Your Team Up for Success

You are the rainmaker, the tribal leader. You have superpower sales and leadership ability that they need and want. They need you to bring in the bacon, bring in the business so they can execute and deliver. One really really important strategy when it comes to sales and execution is keeping your product or service simple and repeatable. If you have too many flavors to what you're trying to do, it makes it harder for the customer to buy off your menu, and it makes it harder for your team to deliver.

Like Chet Holmes says, I would rather do eight things 12,000 times, not 12,000 things eight times. Keep your process and systems predictable and repeatable. The tighter you can make, create, sell, and execute your product the more competitive advantage and sales you can make.

One of the competitive advantages we had, because our process and product were consistent and simple, was that we could deliver 50% faster than the market average and our product outperformed competitors. Talk about meeting the needs of the customer, saving them money, and getting quality. You get a lot more buys and bulk buys when you can show you do it over and over again. You're a trusted partner. And this is highly motivating for your team. They get to know, learn, and love serving the client. They can learn to anticipate what they need because they're so in sync, and they can offer solutions in real-time when the client has fires that come up. It's important for your team to be in touch with the customers the business serves. Magical things happen when everyone feels important and empowered to carry out their role in producing the result you want.

Recognize and Praise Your Team

Do it often! One of my favorite organizational culture gurus, Chester Elton, says "Why hold back?" Is too much praise too much? Not if it's earned. Praise multiple times a day. Do you understand what they're going to say when they go home? That'll be one of the best days of their year. Build up your team with the affirmations that we talked about, help them believe more in themselves. Help them see what you see in them, which is they are incredibly talented and vital assets to the business. They are appreciated and valued. When you live your life and then show and reflect it onto them, you build massive traction and buy in.

On my office whiteboard, we had a list of personal milestones mapped out for each person. Every time one of us hit one, we'd celebrate. They were big milestones too, and we hit every single one of them for over two years. It was so awesome to see and use that simple list as proof of progress, growth, and success. I recommend having something like this set up in your office for your team to see over time.

Can you hit your company's KPIs with this approach? You bet they can! You want to get to the point where your team is self-managed because you're teaching them EQ, personal development, gratitude, and affirmations. Over time, you should have them come to you and they will tell you what their problem is and what solutions they're considering to implement to change the situation. Self-managed. Not micromanagement. Most people do not like micromanagement, and you will push them away, fast. Hire the right people, and instill the right culture, be the tribal leader they need you to be. They will respect and respond to you and follow you to the end.

You'll know through EQ when there are times that you need to support, motivate, reprimand, encourage, teach, etc. It's a learning process. But all this is what I mean by leading with radical integrity. It's being vulnerable, it's authentic, it's raw honesty, it's specific and focused, it's safe, it's creating an environment to learn and grow, but always doing the right thing. It's accountable. It's fun.

Exercise: What are the values your team has? Do this with them, not for them. What do you all want to stand for? Write down three to five things and see if that's the type of culture you want to create. Then go live it.

Once you understand how to practice gratitude and radical integrity with your team, it's hard to not find the office a more rewarding place to be. Raise the next leaders with this approach, help them become amazing fathers and moms, husbands and wives, friends. Make work enjoyable, enriching, a safe place to learn and grow, to compete and win, a place where they can achieve all their goals. They win, and you win.

> *It's not about you, it never was. It gets to be you, to impact the lives of your team and your clients. You get to be the tribal leader everyone wanted but never had, until you came along. It's about them. Go make them great, by being great.*
>
> – JAMES JACOBI

CHAPTER 10

Serve Your Family First, Last, and Foremost

The difference of my home life today versus five to seven years ago is astounding. Well, yes, we had three children in that period of time, so that certainly changes things. But before, my foundation, defense systems, and influences sucked. I had no chance of making it long-term with poor strategies, not practicing gratitude, and not using affirmations and meditation to form my mind and help me become my best self. My choice of influencers was poor, so much so that I let it affect my life and my family.

I remember the times when I came home to Lindsay from work, completely burnt out and frustrated, just crying out of total helplessness. That happened several times over those years. That, plus the Ferris wheel of our budget conversations and no faith life, meant we were not in a good place. I mean, we had fun and there were good moments, but in retrospect, we were in trouble.

When you have your babies, priorities and needs change. You need to show up for your family at home as much or more than you do at work. Shut off work when you are home. Please, please do this. Og Mandino talks about this in The Greatest Salesman in the World. It's a paradox, but do not carry the concerns of the work into the home, and do not carry the concerns of home into the workplace. They both deserve their sacred space. Be fully devoted to your spouse and kids when you are home. Remember, tomorrow is never promised, and their youth is fleeting. Kiss them and hug them as much as you can. I have some friends that had their dream come true happen and then be snatched away in a flash. They had twin babies, a boy and a girl. They were born too early. It was not preventable, and they had a few hours of life before both babies took their last breath, dying in their parents' arms. So so sad. Perspective people, get perspective. I don't know how you move on from that, but you find a way. You never forget though and it will always hurt. I've watched my aunt, for fourteen years now, mourn the death of her only son and child, Ryan. He was my cousin and we grew up together. We were close, and we shared the silliest of memories together.

He was incredibly humble and always put others first. He was a Marine reserve and was called to serve his country in Fallujah, Iraq, in 2004. He was only there three months and never returned. My grandparents were incredible. I have such joyful memories and they were a major positive influence on me. My grandfather especially, he disrupted the dental industry in the 1960s, writing two books and doing tours around the world at industry conferences on how to effectively do practice management in your dentist office. He taught dentists how to run their passion as a business that thrived. Talk to anyone from back then who was a dentist, they know him. They traveled the world and lived their dreams. I lost my grandparents to a pilot who took down Flight 990 from JFK International to Egypt in 1999 off Nantucket Island. One of the few things they found in the wreckage was my senior high school picture.

I had clinical depression for three years from those losses and it's why it took me eight years to get my college degree. I was lost, dumbfounded, in a black hole of hurt, loss, and self-pity. I grew addictions to gambling, drinking, and online video games. They were all stalls to not deal with life, to put everything on hold. Most of us have a story like that. We have pain and trauma from something or someone. You need to be authentic and share your life. The good and the bad. It brings people out of hiding and into a safe place. One of my new favorite friends and mentors, Jason Sisneros, who is the founder of Anton Jae Global and owner of seven companies, practices radical integrity so well. He's authentic and truthful, through and through. He lives his words and invites others to join what he calls misfit nation. #misfitnation. He reminds me of one of my favorite movies ever, The Greatest Showman with Hugh Jackman who represents Barnum. Barnum showed the world that the misfits in us or around us, hiding in the shadows, are beautiful and glorious. You can love fully, alive right now today with who you are. Celebrate life and enjoy companionship with others. We are meant to be compassionate, caring, and banding together creatures. In your family life, and at work, and in society. When you start implementing these strategies in this book, your views and perspectives will shift. I cannot wait for you to see what is revealed to you. The beauty within you and in others who are around you.

You'll see the difference when you start practicing gratitude and choosing your words wisely at home. Giving them your full attention. They notice, see it, and feel it. They need you to be their tribal leader at home. What are your values, mission, and vision at home? Oh yeah, that exists too. You have a home culture just like an office culture.

What do you want for your family? How do you want to live out your days together? What does it look like? What's the brand of your family? Who cares what others think? Raise your family your way and do what you think is right for them. They're yours, nobody else's. I say that because I know we all have family or friends that want to tell us how to live our lives. We need to gently say, "I got this, thank you for your input. I'll consider it when needed."

One of the more impactful family decisions I made recently was to deal with the issue that our family spiritual life was dead. We never went to church and always made excuses. When I finally manned up and went out to find the right church for us, that I knew would meet our needs, everything changed. My kids are getting to learn about their spiritual life, love doing it, and it helps them build their identity in the right places with the right influences. We love the music, and we often play it at home now too. It makes us feel good, sing, dance.

You can do the same. What are the decisions and things you need to deal with to help your family move forward? Use the lessons you've learned here at home, they work the same way.

Health

Don't you want to be around for when your kids grow up? Do you even want to put that to chance? I would hope not. So get your yourself together. Love yourself for wherever you're at in your health and wellness journey. Don't you dare look in that mirror and judge? Be kind to yourself. Get your reasons right first and practice gratitude and affirmations with your health.

I hired trainers and dieticians. I didn't know enough on my own or have the discipline to do and eat the right things. I needed accountability for reporting my exercise and eating habits. Before I fired myself a few years ago, I was at the highest weight of my life. I was the Stay Puft Marshmallow Man in Ghostbusters. I weighed over 250 lbs. and had a 43" waist, probably 25+% body fat. Yeah, not good. Long-term, that weight would put me at severe risk for heart issues, blood pressure, diabetes, and more. Today, I'm at 213 lbs. And a 35" waist with 7.5% body fat. It was a lifestyle change and a decision, but I love how I feel and look, and am extremely healthy for my family.

I've tried every diet and exercise program there is. If you want recommendations on what could help you, body fat please email me, and I'd be happy to suggest some resources for you. I will say you have to invest (spend money) into yourself for your health. But you'll find that you'll just be shifting money from areas where you were once unhealthy to healthy ones.

I bring up health and home life in this book for a reason. Because you are one person, everything is connected. What happens at home affects you at work, what happens at work affects you at home. You can't change personalities or habits throughout your day. You'll literally go crazy. This book has key strategies for having a total shift in the quality and healthiness of your life that provide clear roadmaps to achieving massive success at work and home.

Whatever your dreams are for your family, fight for them. Implement what we've talked about here, and don't care about anyone who wants to get in your way. Just smile and pass them by. Family first, last, and always.

CHAPTER 11

Do You Take the Red Pill or the Blue Pill

How to Guarantee Failure

If you have not seen the movie the "Matrix," I will forgive you, but you are seriously living under a rock. Go rent it and let your mind be blown. In it, a hero named Morpheus shows Neo that he has lived in a false world his entire life, and if he wants to know the truth and the real world, he has to make a choice. The blue pill sends you back to your old life, the one you are in now. The red pill shows you the truth and reveals where you can go.

Let's get real. A lot of this may seem great, maybe it's some things you already know, or maybe they are concepts and changes too big to make right now in your life. I ask you though, what intrigued you to read this book? Where are you at in your life, at this moment? Know I understand that I am also not perfect. What I offer in this book are things that must be practiced for the rest of our lives. They get richer, deeper, and better as you follow the principles I've described to you. Do you want your life to be better than it is right now, in any way? Did you do the exercises in previous chapters? You have to have the Rubicon moment for you. Make the declaration that you will take that step across the river and never look back. Be fully alive, 100% authentically you. We need you, we really do. As my mentor once told me, "It gets to be you if you want it to be." But if you choose not to, the opportunity will go to someone else. It's your choice: do you want the life you really want? You have to choose now.

Let's cover a few reasons, or should I say excuses, as to why you might not do anything with this information:

Fear It Will Take Too Long, and You Don't Have Time

You don't have any time left to live 50% of who you are. You have loved ones depending on you, cheering, and secretly praying for you to be bold, courageous. Your genius is needed. Yes, it will take time to implement and practice and get better. Same as losing 100 lbs. It won't happen overnight. You need to chip away at it, but you create momentum. And momentum, as it builds, will have powers beyond your imagination to what it will do in your life.

Fear of Being Different

This one is just dumb, sorry. And I'm telling myself this too because I was captive to this for a long time in my life. Different is good! Not one single person is the same on this planet, not one. We are all unique, beautiful, wonderfully made. Yes, there are social norms, office norms, politics, political correctness, etc. If any of that is at the expense of you not being you, and living and sticking to what you value, then you've got to get over it. Your different opinions or thoughts or values are needed; they're important.

Fear of Looking Stupid

Look dumb, look so dumb. The only people who think that are judging and insecure of themselves. They are jealous because they didn't have the radical integrity you do to live out loud and display your values naked for everyone to see. You are the tribal leader; your people want to follow you and need your leadership. Just be you!

You've Tried Something like This Before, and It Didn't Work

Failure is not an option. You can't quit because you failed one time or ten times. This is a creed for living differently the rest of your life. You can master these skills and see massive impact. It 100% will happen.

Let's consider the reverse. What is the impact if you make no change to your situation at work and at home? Are you running closer to having success as a leader, growing your sales, growing a tribe, growing a family tribe, or is it escaping you?

Don't wait until it hurts more or until you get permission. Many of us want to wait for some magical permission from the universe to go be great. Don't wait to meet the biggest influencer that you value so they can tell you the same thing I'm telling you now. And don't wait for something tragic like cancer or loss of life to be the tipping point for you. Choose now, act now.

If your stress on a daily or weekly basis is high right now, that is not sustainable with the results you're getting. You might as well have a lot of stress playing a much bigger game. Burn the boats for where you are, say no more. Go all in emotionally, financially, mentally, and spiritually to move forward.

One of the things that made a massive difference for me in making all these changes and implementing them, was having support and accountability. This journey is not meant to go alone, you have many many people that want to support you and go through this together with you. If you are interested in joining a group of like-minded people that will support you, hold you accountable and not judge you, check out my private Facebook group: *Radical Integrity Community Group*. It's a place where like-minded people want to transform their business, sales and life with integrity.

Further, if you feel like it would be beneficial to do some one on one coaching, let's talk. With my ninety-day program, I will walk you through all of this. I want to see you win, grow, be all of you. Message me at james@jamesjacobi.com and say, "I'm in." We'll get a call set up to get started from there.

BONUS GOODIES JUST FOR YOU!

Go to **www.jamesjacobi.com/goodies** for secret access to 4 pieces of training on:

1. Taking the First Step - Becoming the Leader Within
2. Know Your Value - How to Become the Expert Your Client Needs
3. Show Your Value - How to Outshine Your Competition
4. Force Your Win - How to Have Unshakable Confidence and Close Business

If you want more help, book a call with me now. Just visit **https://JamesJacobi.as.me/**

YOU CANNOT FIND THIS PAGE FROM MY WEBSITE. IT'S A SECRET BETWEEN YOU AND ME, HERE. IT'S WORTH THOUSANDS OF DOLLARS, BUT FOR YOU IT'S FREE. I WANT TO HELP YOU WIN, RIGHT NOW, WHERE YOU ARE AT. YOU'VE GOT THIS! :-)

CONCLUSION

What Happens Now?

I know it's scary out there and the weight of the world can feel so unbelievably heavy on you. You have a ton of responsibilities and a lot of people depending on you. You can and will be an amazing leader. Just start implementing the SUCCESS steps and watch what happens. In ninety days, heck in as few as seven days, you'll begin to see a difference. Once you do that, imagine it as your new lifestyle.

Don't do this alone. Find a mentor, a success coach. Find a mastermind of talented individuals that can sharpen your iron. I learned so much from the group of people I collaborated with on the Bora Bora trip, and similar circles of influence. You learn and grow so much with shared wisdom and knowledge. That is the point. They're meant to scale and teach you things faster than anywhere else, so you can grow and see results. Your mind will unlock and show you things you've never seen before. You will be equipped to help so many more people in a much better way. If you would like to work with me one on one or get information on my private mastermind group, please contact me at james@jamesjacobi.com and say "I'm in."

One last thing, forgiveness. You may have a very painful present and past. I learned some incredible things from Pastor Tim Lucas about what forgiveness really means. It doesn't mean to forget, you can remember, and you will. It doesn't mean to downplay the offense. It was valid and your hurt or anger is justified. It does mean you have a choice. Forgiveness is not meant to pardon the person who offended you, but it's meant for you to let go, so you can move on. Without forgiveness, you live in the past. You need to be fully in the present, building your dream for tomorrow. You are where you are today from the decisions you made. Forgive yourself, and forgive whomever you need to, because you need to move on, and start this journey forward.

> *"Everyone thinks of changing the world,*
> *but no one thinks of changing himself."*
> —LEO TOLSTOY

As Jay Samit discusses in his book Disrupt You, Jay talks about the requirement that you must transform yourself first before you are able to change the world.

Disruptors see that they can make the world different, in a more positive way, by being an agent of change. To change the world, you must change first. Jay describes this process as de-constructing a set of assumptions so as to disrupt a problem and thereby create a new opportunity. If you are able to deconstruct problems in your own life and in your habits, it will give you an opportunity to create new habits that serve you well. As an exercise, Jay recommends writing down 3 problems a day that needs to be solved for 30 days. You will soon learn how to see and identify problems that you could disrupt with a new solution. By doing so, you will know what needs evaluation and change for your own sales and leadership goals which will transform your business, teams, and life.

As you go on this path of development and growth, your brand, influence, leadership, and sales mastery will rise, and your tribe will form and follow. Practice gratitude. Live with courageous and radical integrity, and raw loving honesty. You will build the most trusted relationships you'll ever have, and magical things will happen. You will be a successful sales leader for your business and your family.

BONUS GOODIES JUST FOR YOU!

Go to **www.jamesjacobi.com/goodies** for secret access to 4 pieces of training on:

1. Taking the First Step - Becoming the Leader Within
2. Know Your Value - How to Become the Expert Your Client Needs
3. Show Your Value - How to Outshine Your Competition
4. Force Your Win - How to Have Unshakable Confidence and Close Business

If you want more help, book a call with me now. Just visit **https://JamesJacobi.as.me/**

YOU CANNOT FIND THIS PAGE FROM MY WEBSITE. IT'S A SECRET BETWEEN YOU AND ME, HERE. IT'S WORTH THOUSANDS OF DOLLARS, BUT FOR YOU IT'S FREE. I WANT TO HELP YOU WIN, RIGHT NOW, WHERE YOU ARE AT. YOU'VE GOT THIS! :-)

FURTHER READING

Sell or Be Sold by Grant Cardone

Disrupt You by Jay Samit

Tribes by Seth Goden

Greatest Salesman in the World by Og Mandino

I Choose Joy by Danelle Delgado

Authority Marketing by Justin Blatt

Crush It by Gary Vaynerchuk

Crushing It by Gary Vaynerchuk

Maxout by Ed Mylett

Mastery by Robert Greene

Success Principles by Jack Canfield

ACKNOWLEDGMENTS

This book idea came together over the last two years of my finding my authentic identity and leadership. It's a testament to leaping with faith into uncharted waters, many many times, and trusting in something bigger than me that came to be my calling. It's a testament to taking action, no matter how big or crazy the task is, and implementing to learn and grow.

The moment I said yes to reaching out to influencers and highly successful people in business and life, there was a pull that could not stop. I wanted the best for my marriage and family, and I knew I had to learn, study, practice, implement, and keep taking action to change the trajectory of our lives. Had it not been for Grant Cardone's 10x conference where my wife and I met Danelle Delgado, we may never have arrived here. Danelle opened the floodgates of new learnings, a world of ambitious, kind, generous, integrity, and genius people that we'd one day call friends. I've learned so much from you and my transformation to becoming the one my results require would not have been possible without you.

To Danny, Zak, and Dylan for having the faith and trust to do the things we did together to grow our business and team to unfounded heights. You are a huge part to my being able to write this story and teachings that will help so many. You are all incredible men of character and talent.

To Angela Kubisky and Paul Boudreau at the Morris County Regional Chamber of Commerce. Your faith in me to provide value and insights to the business community and be on the board has introduced me to so many profound leaders. It led me to Tim Lucas, who has helped me and my family find a church home that has radically improved our faith life.

To Angela Lauria. The moment I saw your YouTube video, I just knew you were the one. I had wanted to write a book, share my story, but didn't really know how. You have literally paved the way and have equipped me to serve the millions I hope to impact with my message. I have learned so much about how to write a book and run a business that matters.

To my wife, Lindsay. You have been with me through hardest of times and back. Your love, commitment, faith, trust, and openness to what's possible has been an incredible journey in our marriage, faith, and life. I'm so blessed and grateful that we've made these leaps to live our dreams together. I pray God will bless us to serve and impact so many through our inspirations.

To the Morgan James Publishing team: Special thanks to David Hancock, CEO & Founder for believing in me and my message. To my Author Relations Manager, Gayle West, thanks for making the process seamless and easy. Many more thanks to everyone else, but especially Jim Howard, Bethany Marshall, and Nickcole Watkins.

THANK YOU

Thank you to The Author Incubator team, my mentors and influencers, my brother Steve for always being there to support me, my career colleagues for providing me the experiences, relationships, and opportunities that have prepared me for what's next, my parents, and family members for teaching me so many life lessons that have shaped me in character, and my wife, Lindsay. None of this would have happened without you all. Thank you for allowing me to share my story, wisdom, and business and life lessons, so that we can touch the lives of our future leaders. May we help and empower them to live boldly, as heroes, with integrity and gratitude.

ABOUT THE AUTHOR

James Jacobi is the founder of Jacobi Enterprises, LLC and Magic Moment Fund (a 501c3 nonprofit charity). He is the author of the bestselling book *Radical Integrity: 7 Breakthrough Strategies for Transforming Your Business, Sales, and Life.*

He is a bestselling author, successful entrepreneur, and motivational speaker. He's a six-time president's club winner, a recognized millennial leader on multiple boards of directors and has shared stages at top business conferences with Danelle Delgado, Tim Grover, and Roddy Chong.

James has spent the last 10 years in corporate working with small business to Fortune 100 firms. James has held senior business development and operational leadership roles while being the top producer amidst

300+ producers. He knows how to help scale a small business to one of the largest companies in the industry. He understands the challenges middle management faces to run highly effective teams.

In his book *Radical Integrity*, James details the mental strategies it takes to be a consistent high producing asset and influencer, how to grow sales by 400% in 90 days, create high performing teams without turnover, use modern customer centric business strategies, and how to carry those same strategies into having a happy home life. He specializes in helping sales leaders in small and large businesses become the aspired leader within. He lives in Randolph, New Jersey. with his wife Lindsay, and three children Grant, Willa and George.

JAMES CAN BE REACHED VIA:

Website: www.jamesjacobi.com
Email: james@jamesjacobi.com
Instagram: @realjamesjacobi
Facebook: james.jacobi
LinkedIn: linkedin.in/jamesjacobi
Twitter: @jamesjacobi